AF531795

GREAT EXPECTATIONS AND GRIM REALITIES IN EDUCATIONAL SCENARIO

GREAT EXPECTATIONS AND GRIM REALITIES IN EDUCATIONAL SCENARIO

A Compendium of Issues

By

Dr. S. DANDAPANI, M.A., M.Ed., Ph.D.
Formerly Professor in Educational Psychology,
Regional College of Education
Mysore-570006
(NCERT)

ANMOL PUBLICATIONS PVT. LTD.
NEW DELHI - 110 002 (INDIA)

ANMOL PUBLICATIONS PVT. LTD.
4374/4B, Ansari Road, Daryaganj
New Delhi - 110 002
Ph.: 23261597, 23278000
Visit us: www.anmolpublications.com

Great Expectations and Grim Realities in Educational Scenario

First Edition, 2003

ISBN 81-261-1553-X

PRINTED IN INDIA

Published by J.L. Kumar for Anmol Publications Pvt. Ltd., New Delhi - 110 002 and Printed at Tarun Offset Press, Delhi.

Dedicated

to

My Teachers and Students

"THERE IS A GREAT DEAL OF DIFFERENCE BETWEEN THE EAGER MAN WHO WANTS TO READ A BOOK AND THE TIRED MAN WHO WANTS A BOOK TO READ."

G.K. CHESTERTON.

Contents

Individual Differences

Research

Education Reforms

Teacher as Role Model

Teaching Strategies

Mental Health

Other Issues

Preface

Thoughts are like butterflies. Their movement and direction are unpredictable. They seldom stay long enough to watch and study. Being aware of the nature of thoughts one has to capture them as they appear.

Education is an investment. We invest time, effort, money- almost everything we value. We must reap the benefits. Our future rests on the solid foundation laid by our preceptors and parents.

Aldous Huxley observes: "Perhaps the most valuable result of all education is the ability to do the thing you have to do when it ought to be done, whether you like it or not. However early a man's training begins it is probably the last lesson that he learns thoroughly."

A teacher has to be creative, caring, committed and conscientious. Teacher is watched by several pairs of eyes for years. It behoves a teacher to fulfil the expectations of students.

Obstacles are stepping stones to success. While the weak-minded stumble and crumble, the strong-willed confront and conquer.

Blessed are those who are not only informed but also transformed.

Best wishes,

S. DANDAPANI

1

Concepts of Schooling

A time has come for us to consider calmly the concept of schooling. If one were to ask a parent, the response would be more or less like this: "School is an institution meant for providing adequate knowledge and information that would enable a student to secure an appropriate slot in society ensuring a decent, comfortable living." Few would disagree with such a pious expectation. How would a teacher view schooling? Regardless of shades of differences, most teachers tend to look upon schooling as an institutionalised information centre, to provide basic skills in acquiring knowledge in a time-frame under the guidance and supervision of qualified personnel leading to a certificate or degree as a proof of acquiring proficiency." This view appears more formalised, precise and explicit. Again, such a conception too would not be disputed.

Let us pose this question to the very consumer of the commodity, viz., student. We tend to underestimate, the maturity of a learner, to be aware of her/his goal or destination. Yet, we "have to" know their point of view, at least to ward off the accusation that they were led blind-folded. Some are vociferously vocal to assert their right to have a "say". Ask a primary schooler. The reply would be "To have fun, to meet fellow-learners, to forge friendship, to be away from home at least for a few hours, to feel free to observe as well as violate man-made rules and regulations, to acquire fundamental skills of learning rather spontaneously than under coercion or threat." Though these kids may not use such precise expression, they would convey such ideas.

By the time a learner ascends to the high-school stage, he/she gets accustomed to accept unquestioningly most of what they are taught in class. They tend to equate schooling with racing wherein losers would always outnumber gainers. They begin to doubt the existence of terms such as "Scientific temper", "Rationality", "Morality", 'Integrity', 'Equity', 'Aesthetics' and "common-sense". Except for occasional references in Educational seminars and confernece, these worthy ideals rarely percolate into practical reality.

How does a psychologist view schooling? Very rarely his/her views are elicited or valued. The psychologist is considered a utopian, one who espouses the cause of the young at the expense of the old. He shares the fate of Socrates. Yet, a few are emboldened to air their views. "Allow a child to be a child", "Facilitate learning rather than imparting all the time", "Accept children unconditionally rather than rewarding the gifted and punishing the less-gifted". "Experiment pupil-teacher planning than the teacher planning for pupils".

In short, make schooling a memorable voyage of discovery-learning that would remain as permanent imprints in their psyche and not as a trauma to be gone through inescapably. How many of us have the will to face reality?

2

Premature Preschooling

Schooling is the second home for a child. In other words, a child has to feel at home in a school. What is a home? It is a place where a child feels secure, accepted and loved unconditionally. There is no discrimination among siblings. A mother treats each child impartially and loves whole heartedly. The first word uttered by a baby fills the parents with a good deal of pride and pleasure. Perhaps their first-born might have shown some precocity, while the second or third might show slightly delayed development. Nevertheless, each child, assuming the children to be reasonably normal, demostrates a predictable sequence of development. In this competition-free environment, every child enjoys spontaneous growth and progress.

Let us examine what happens to a child when shifted to a preschool-setting. First and foremost, it is an abrupt transition from the familiar, homely surroundings to a relatively strange atmosphere. Naturally it fills the child with predictable uneasiness. Every parent would vouchsafe the turmoil she had to undergo to make her baby accept the new teacher, and accommodate to the new environment. Regardless of the posh building, bright uniforms, plush school-van, and benign teacher, babies do resent—if not reject the transition.

It looks as though the present-day parents have had enough of the "pesterings" of children who might be unduly curious to know every little thing around, or inordinately hungry, all day long particularly for home-made sweets'. Perhaps they make the life of a housewife pretty miserable. But, the question is, are we as parents, more interested in packing off these little Newtons and Edisons to some school for a few hours so that we could concentrate on cooking, house-keeping or watching a TV serial? Have we found these little creatures an interminable, nuisance to rob us of a little privacy? Have we become so fatigued so soon and so early to be free from their innocent pranks and, of course, their temper-tantrums as well?

It is true that most pre-schools we find today do not and cannot be an effective substitute for the warmth of a home. A few might boast of a conducive environment. But, even in such places, something is missing that even a child from the humblest of homes, misses very badly. This is not to denounce the pre-schools or their teachers. I only question the rationale of pre-schooling. Are we inadvertently abdicating our duties and responsibilities as parents who should be the primary educators of our own creations? Rightly, said, every home should be a pre-school.

"Laughter is the sun that drives winter from the human face"

—*Victor Hugo.*

3

Teaching: Professionalism, Not Professing

A sweeping change has engulfed business and banking. Sick industries are either closed or streamlined by infusing modern technology and augmenting productivity. "Progress or perish" is the watchword of the emerging millennium.

An age-old profession such as Teaching can never rest on oars grinding the same old archaic , arm-chair methods. It is time we gave a shock-treatment to the lotus-eaters who were counting their pay and perquisites than being committed to the process of educating learners. The reason is the guaranteed tenure when once the probationary period is crossed plus the substandard appraisal of the Inspectorate in evaluating the performance of teachers in classrooms.

The reservation policy has come in the way of maintaining standards of teaching at the entry level as well as promotional prospects. One could cite instances of conscientious teachers being given a raw deal, while the perfunctory performers getting away with undeserved advantages!

Schools can be deemed to be the mega industry responsible for the generation of human resources to improve the quality of life in the country. The backwardness of a country can be traced to the education-system that is in vogue.

Educational administrators are more concerned with larger allocation of funds in the budget rather than fine-tuning the instruction in classrooms. Laboratories, libraries, classrooms, play-fields and other infrastructural facilities, by themselves, do not guarantee quality education if the teachers were to shirk their duties and responsibilities.

There is no ISO certification for schools, to my knowledge. Categorising schools on the basis of percentage of passes is not a valid rating. Some schools refuse to admit the average and below average and entertain only students with superior mental abilities.

A systematic coaching is done months ahead of the Public examination and a reflex-like answering to the Information loaded questions is practised systematically. No wonder all the horses breast the winning tape together.

Millions of schools do not join the race because the teachers are assured of their increment regardless of examination-result. They couldn't care less as the students remained indifferent in class.

Is there a way out of this impasse? Not that we have a ready-made, magical solution at hand. We could conjecture a few. In every school there should be a "Quality Circle" similar to the ones found in Japanese Industries. The Head of the Institution should be dynamic as well as dedicated to give of his best as well as getting the best out of everyone of his colleagues. At least once in a month he/she should convene an all-faculty meet on a saturday afternoon.

This is not for empty exhortation or witch-hunting but to transact the business of ensuring Quality-teaching. Teachers could form groups subject-wise and do a kind of brainstorming. They could share their secrets of success and failure with a few to benefit from frank and fearless discussion.

The Headmaster could join any group or move from group to group to make sure that time is not wasted on frivolous issues. After a short tea-break the teachers could assemble and each group could present whatever they discussed and arrived at. The entire proceedings must be mimeographed and circulated to the staff.

It is also worthwhile to invite the parents twice in an academic year to hear their views for the betterment of instruction. Let us understand that schools are agencies set up by the community to educate the younger members and make them useful, productive citizens of the nation. Instead of allowing tempers to rise and indulging in mutual recrimination, teachers should observe restraint and make parents realise they are joint-partners in the education of the youth.

If some educated parents volunteer to supplement instruction by sharing their expertise, the school authorities must avail this offer.

Why should we not involve students too in this quality-improvement? Bright students in each class should be identified and guided to guide their classmates who were lagging behind. This kind of cooperative endeavour is far better than the cut-throat competition practised in schools. Team-spirit is superior to individual excellence. Would this not result in Total Quality Management (TQM) of schools? Am I a utopian or a pragmatist? If we do not dream, we should languish in ugly reality.

4

The Ups and Downs of Hierarchy

We have grown accustomed to perceive those perched atop as the citadels of learning- "Professors in Universities", as paragons of excellence, erudition and exemplary conduct. Indeed it was true of quite a few luminaries decades ago!

Over the years the metal has lost its sheen and faded considerably, presumably because we have allowed all and sundry to occupy this unique chair regardless of one's accomplishment.

Have we carried this label "Professor" to its etymological extreme? "To profess" means "to pretend", to be insincere and to put on a facade of loftiness and to conceal hollowness. If the word "Professor" is said to be a derivative of the verb "to profess", then most people who now have the dubious distinction of being named "Professors" richly deserve this uncomplimentary prefix. It has become increasingly difficult to discriminate the meritorious from the mediocrites.

Assuming that those who manage to ascend the hierarchy do deserve a little of what they claim as their legitimate due, let us analyse their day-to-day duties and responsibilities. They are supposed to devote themselves to a deep study and research in a specified branch, share their findings and expertise with their colleagues as well as students, facilitate learning and promote research of a higher order. Professors who conform to these requirements are barely a few in our country. Those few who plough the lonely furrow, far from public glare, seldom parade their accomplishments. They remain unrecognised and unrewarded. The hollow ones contrive to rise by fair or foul means and their extroverted behaviour catapults them to dizzy heights!

These professors receive handsome pay and several nominations to University Bodies like the Senate and the Syndicate. In terms of teaching work-load these worthies usually have a few hours per week. There is no guarantee that they would make their presence in classrooms, not, to speak of interaction with students beyond class hours'. They invariably have a heavy schedule of Examinerships, Board-meetings, Extension-lectures, Selection-committee Meetings etc. Yet, they remain on the pay-roll of the University. They are always looked upto for all kinds of inaugurations and valedictions. Of course they deliver (read out) pompous speeches.

What about those humble ones, who sweat themselves out in ill-ventilated, crowded classrooms to transmit the rudimentary skills of acquiring knowledge? They invariably become caricatures for cartoonists, convenient messengers to do census work, election duties, and similar "national" service. They are periodically sermonised to be duty-conscious, creative in teaching, scrupulous in correcting exercise books, inculcating in tender minds a taste for fine arts, proficiency in games and sports and so on by the headmaster as well as the Inspectorate. While their prescribed duty is to teach what is found in textbooks, their unspecified duties are legion. They seldom realise that what they perform is of primary importance even though they teach primary classes!

Those who teach in high-schools tend to assume more wisdom than those teaching in lower classes. Paradoxically, as the students proceed to higher classes, the teachers have lesser necessity to bestow individualised attention. However they receive a heavier pay-packet for their superior qualitative work than those in the lower rungs!

The whole bunch of them are fading into insignificance in comparison with those lecturing in colleges. Of course we find in the summit Professors of Eminence, who perhaps, might be looking upto some of their privileged colleagues, elevated as Vice-Chancellors. In a hierarchy, we cannot help looking up and looking down. So long as we don't look down upon those in the lower rungs, there is no harm in looking up. After all, we cannot think of the superstructure, without a strong solid base-foundation!

"The righteous promise little and perform much; the wicked promise much and perform not even a little."

—*Babylonian.*

"When about to commit a base dead respect thyself, though there is no witness."

— *Anacharsis.*

5

Is Elementary Education Really Elementary ?

The innumerable reforms, schemes and projects that have almost inundated high schools and higher institutions have more or less left the area of elementary education to the elements of Nature. The enigmatic title, elementary education is, in itself, a proof of the callous indifference and step-motherly treatment it has been accorded. Is elementary education really elementary? To me, the term 'Primary Education' seems to be a more appropriate one.

Primary education carries with it a responsibility of primary importance. Since the foundation of one's personality is laid at the earliest stage, are we not bound to bestow greater care and attention at the base than trimming the superstructure? At present we are working on an edifice built on a sandy soil and raise a hue and cry when gets tilted at the top.

If we conduct a survey of the number of elementary schools in our country that can boast of a decent building, good classroom and the minimum equipment needed to teach, we would find quite a microscopic minority. The appalling conditions of the upkeep of elementary schools need no elaboration. And these are the clearing houses of the future citizens of our country. A few prestigious schools like the Convents are only drops in the ocean, catering to the drops of the upper income groups.

Every state department of education conducts an annual survey of the enrolment of pupils at the elementary stage to feed a bulky volume brought out by the Central Ministry of Education. The statistics is quite impressive. Has the increase in intake kept pace with the capacity of the schools in terms of staff and equipment? To a great extent the existing resources are deployed to meet the teeming millions of children thronging at the primary schools.

What is the role of parents? Majority of them drive their children to school not with the zeal and commitment to get them enlightened by education, but simply to be rid of their nuisance at home for sometime atleast. The children are impounded within the four walls of an ill-ventilated cell called classroom, and a care-taker in the garb of a teacher has to tame them. Quite an assortment of kids emerging from varied socio-economic background meet there to receive mutual reinforcement for their impetuosity. The teacher is very much like a ringmaster, moving around the class, brandishing a cane to keep them quiet. At least a circus ringmaster refuses to manage beyond a few animals at a time, while an elementary school teacher has not only to manage a single class of overwhelming strength but also perform another feat known as "Multi-class Teaching." Like Lord Maha Vishnu, he has to be everywhere simultaneously!

Every time I read the writings of Montessori, Froebel, Pestalozzi and Piaget, I used to feel like a diplomatic visitor going around on a conducted tour. Worse still, when I had to lecture on the contributions of such great educational thinkers, I would feel as though I lived in a fool's, paradise. It would be just like speaking on the nutritive values of apples and peaches when you can't even afford a banana!

Leaving aside the fancy toys and materials with which a convent classroom is stuffed can't we guarantee our children a comfortable desk and bench, a really black board and an enthusiastic, lovable teacher. Is our country so poor as to deny the millions of children the bare necessities of education at the elementary stage?

I don't know whose brain-wave it was, that a matriculate is good enough to manage an elementary class. There cannot be a greater fallacy than this. To make a child understand such meaningless symbols as 'alphabet' and use them to understand arbitrary combinations known as 'words' and make them master a whole lot of grammatical gymnastics, require a more mature brain than that of a matriculate. Why not, for a change, a University Professor step into an elementary class and see for himself whether teaching them is really elementary?

"We are all in the same boat in a stormy sea, and we owe each other a terrible loyalty."

—*G.K. Chesterton.*

"Only a fool tests the depth of the water with both feet."

— *African Proverb.*

6

Pleasures of Reading

Among the three R's, reading has been accorded the prime position. Right from Primary grades we are taught "how to read" as well as "how not to read". Children are delighted to hear the teacher reading out a story. It could be the story of the fox that could not reach the bunch of grapes or the story of Archimedes running naked through the streets of Syracuse, shouting "Eureka, Eureka." Watch the faces of children intently watching every gesture of the teacher when she read out a Panchatantra tale or an episode from the Mahabaratha. Unless a teacher enjoyed reading she cannot make children enjoy listening. The joy is infectious. The teacher demonstrates and trains children in the art of reading. Every child must experience the thrill of reading aloud. This would afford an opportunity for the teacher to train children in proper pronunciation, intonation, pause, stress and exclamation. Children welcome such opportunities, because every child aspires to emulate the teacher.

Reading for pleasure precedes reading with a purpose. The transition has to be smooth and not abrupt. Compulsory reading is likely to create resentment. As students move up to high-school classes the pace of reading gathers momentum. The choice of reading also undergoes change. They are no more excited by fairy-tales. They might enjoy real life adventures. Readers' Digest regularly publish an article, titled,

"Drama in real life". Sometimes informative articles can be informally and interestingly presented. J. D. Radcliff is one such fascinating writer of 'Popular Science' articles. His articles on, "I am John's glands" present a lot of scientific facts in the first person singular style. By the time children reach high-school classes they would have cultivated the art of silent reading. Silent reading can be more enjoyable than reading aloud. Moreover, it contributes to rapid reading. The whole class can be allowed to read stories or essays from different books or magazines for about twenty minutes. Each one may be asked to relate what they have read and grasped. Teachers should resist the temptation to correct their grammatical mistakes in an offensive manner. It should be done subtly, unobtrusively. The student should not feel hurt. When a student approaches the teacher at the end of the class and says, "Thank you, Sir. I am glad you corrected me. I might have persisted reporting wrongly". We seldom realise how much we owe to our teachers who guided and shaped us during our formative years!

We need to have a perennial supply of reading materials for providing opportunities to children to learn to read. That means, we have to have a number of writers. We should understand that every writer must have been a reader in the beginning. It is by constant reading that one acquires rich vocabulary. A dictionary contains more words than most of us know. We do not have to know all the words. As and when we come across an unfamiliar word, we refer a dictionary. That would be a mere acquaintance. To be more familiar with a new word we should come across-the new word, experience a hazy memory, refer the dictionary once again and thus establish friendship. However, the new word becomes a close friend only when we use it while writing or speaking. It is really amazing that in our brain we have accommodated so many words.

Everyone aspires to be a good writer. Writing is a discipline. We need to venture and try. Like swimming, we have to get into the river or swimming pool, struggle, survive and succeed. The earlier it is commenced, the better. All writers have followed this principle. Overnight one cannot become a celebrated writer like R.K. Narayan. One does not need a string of degrees to be an eminent writer. R.K. Narayan studied only upto B.A. But, he had an irrepressible urge to write. His brother, on the other hand, had an uncontrollable urge to sketch cartoons. The two brothers have developed their gifts. Many more Narayans and Laxmans remain unrecognised in many a classroom. One can go on writing about reading and writing. A writer is a photographer. He evokes the imagery very vividly. As one reads one also visualises. Here is a passage from Ruskin Bond, a nature-lover, who lives in a wooden Cabin at Simla:

"When the monsoon brings the first rains of summer, the parched Earth opens its pores and quenches its thirst with a hiss of ecstasy. After baking in the sun for the last few months, the land looks cracked, dusty and tired. Now, almost overnight, new grass springs up, there is renewal everywhere, and the damp earth releases fragrance sweeter than any devised by man".

My purpose in writing this article is to awaken your urge to read and write and not all the time sit before a computer, pressing the keys and watching the screen. Exercise your inert muscles, enjoy writing and reading as your father and grandfather did in their days.

7

Viable Teacher-Training

Once upon a time Teacher-training colleges were very few in our country. Not many knocked at the doors of these. Over the past two decades there appears to be a boom in this domain, judging by the mushroom proliferation of Teacher-training Institutions as well as Institutes of correspondence courses. No serious attempt has been made to take stock of the manpower needs of the country and regulate the intake. Quantitative expansion does not seem to ensure commensurate qualitative improvement. By and large, the trainees are given liberal dosage of theories pertaining to pedagogy that bear little relationship to the ground realities of real class-room teaching. It is doubtful whether such a training really benefits the trainees with all the requisite skills and knowledge needed to manage an assortment of kids thronging the class. It is not certain whether all the faculty members who inflict upon the unwary trainees a plethora of principles of Education honestly believe in the efficacy of such theories or simply dole out as a matter of routine. Quite a few would even make it known that the trainees need not swear by what they are taught but evolve on their own a unique mode of instruction! With all these misgivings a prospective teacher embarks on the profession of teaching only to unlearn whatever he had learnt!

It is imperative that the faculty members in a College of Education co-ordinate their efforts and function as a well-knit team and impart teaching skills with a good deal of creative flexibility. Unfortunately, members compartmentalise themselves into specialised areas each one being proficient in one's own domain with dim awareness of the neighbourhood disciplines. Quite often trainees are rather perplexed by the division of labour and find it a gargantuan job to synthesise theories and practices.

A firm foundation on content is the desideratum for becoming a good teacher. There can be no compromise on this. It it were to be so, is it justifiable to admit all and sundry in a Teacher-training institution and dump on them a heavy load of Pedagogical principles? The biggest defaulter here is the system of Correspondence Education that had grown like parthenium and come to stay. A random sample check upon the performance of candidates of correspondence course reveals the utter ineptitude and hollowness. A teacher worth the name has to be reasonably good in expression, to be meaningful to others. Any attempt to make a teacher out of someone who is chronically deficient in linguistic skills is nothing but constructing a structure on a sandy soil! It is bound to collapse.

Every profession has to register a constant upward trend which is possible only when members receive a kind of training that would stimulate them to improve themselves even after training. Unfortunately most of the teaching and evaluation practices sedulously learnt during training are forgotten soon after examination. Micro-teaching is supposedly aimed at the mastering of several sub-skills in a small class with a limited content, integration of these and transfer to a macro-situation. Much more emphasis has to be laid on micro-teaching, particularly in the context of a situation wherein very little screening has been done before admission.

Action-research is another device to encourage innovative teaching practices out of one's own classroom experiences. This is bound to inspire even a teacher of mediocre abilities. Teaching should not be allowed to degenerate into routinised rituals. It is necessary to institute a periodical scrutiny of the curriculum of teaching and prune out all obsolete practices so as to make it more viable and useful.

> "The test of our progress is not whether we add more to the abundance of those who have much; it is whether we provide enough for those who have too little."
>
> —*F.D. Roosevelt.*

> "The resolution to avoid an evil is seldom framed till the evil is so far advanced as to make avoidance impossible."
>
> —*Thomas Hardy.*

8

Arresting the Exodus

We have been witnessing a proliferation of computer training centres in every nook and corner. Self-financing Engineering colleges are also mushrooming. Even here, computer-application courses are in great demand. Medical colleges are also attracting the meritorious as well as those who can afford to pay huge donation. Thanks to the lucrative career prospects in Chartered Accountancy, commerce courses too attract many. In short, the pendulum has swung away from Arts subjects almost irrevocably!

Literature, History Geography, Philosophy and Anthropology have remained ornamental Art galleries in colleges and universities, facing closure for paucity of funds. Those few who choose to join these non-prestigious courses do not seem to be imbued with passion and devotion. At this rate the probability of producing a few Miltons, Panikkars, Radhakrishnans or Raja Ravi Varmas is becoming bleak. How do we arrest this mass exodus of the cream of student-population? Are we to reconcile to the reality helplessly and allow the drift to continue for ever?

Today we need teachers in schools and colleges who could sow the seed of learning for delight and thought. Such teachers ought to be versatile and peruasive enough to impress upon the youngsters that a purely utilitarian kind of education reflecting the market forces is likely to dwarf one's outlook in life.

The scope for individual excellence and creativity is found more in Arts and Literature. As Bertrand Russell warned we need to discourage students from becoming 'Cogs in the wheel'. We need to raise the quality of instruction in such subjects so that students throng the lecture-halls than canteen or cinema-houses. The lackadaisical attitude of students can be corrected only by innovative and inspiring instruction, making libraries the hub of learning.

Unless the teachers themselves are avid readers of good books, how could they hope to become role-models to their students? As G.K. Chesterton said:

> "There is a great deal of difference
> between the eager man who
> wants to read a book and the
> tired man who wants a book to read."

Of course, 'The Hindu' has been arousing such interest among the youth by publishing poems, drawings and short essays in the YOUNG WORLD. We do find budding writers and artists. Do these buds blossom into fragrant flowers or wither away in Higher education as the cross-currents of material gains swallow the innate genius?

Do they remain contented to pursue these fields as hobbies while the best part of their time and energy is sucked by MBA courses and similar utilitarian avocations? The perpetrators of the pernicious practice are none but parents with blinkered vision of education.

If a five or six-digit salary is going to guarantee everlasting bliss in life, everyone has to join the bee-line of these courses. On the other hand, those few born poets and novelists, thinkers and artists need proper nurturing at home and school. Pursuit of literature did not make Mark Twain poorer! He often said "I never let schooling to interfere with my education." If Thomas Gray had not wandered away from the crowd and rested in a country Churchyard, we would never have had a memorable stanza such as:

> "Full many a gem of purest ray serene,
> The dark unfathom'd caves of ocean bear,
> Full many a flower is born to blush unseen
> And waste its sweetness on the desert air."

"Sadness is a wall between two gardens."

— *Khalil Gibran.*

"Hospitality consists in a little fun, a little food and immense quiet."

—*Ralph Waldo Emerson.*

9

Inform or Transform?

Long after my sons and daughters were settled in life, I came across a memorable quotation, "The child today is no longer coming to school to be informed... but to be transformed!" What a prophetic statement! I feel that this golden saying should be displayed in bold letters in every Principal's room in every school. Parents and teachers ought to read this when they admit their children to school.

A plethora of information get generated every day. No school can possibly capsule these and transmit them into the tiny heads of millions of children thronging the classrooms. Time is limited for teaching while knowledge is limitless. We would only be waging a losing battle to conquer and teach everything that children ought to learn. We hear the refrain that knowledge becomes obsolete soon, as it is galloping faster than we can cope with. Quite often teachers are alarmed at the pace of progress in every field. Every publication of Science and Technology Section in "The Hindu" reveals many "Hotlines" and "Medilines" and "Question Corners". Whatever is taught in the past gets reduced to irrelevance soon. With the advent of Information Technology and Internet, youngsters are glued to the small screen to gather knowledge and wisdom.

We are now in a dilemma. Are we to 'inform' or

'transform' a student? Most teachers do the former. Very few attempt the latter. Why? Unless the teacher herself is transformed, it is not possible to transform students. Only a magnetised iron can magnetise other iron pieces. For instance, water gets transformed into vapour or ice-cubes. Seed gets transformed into a plant. Flowers turn into a fruit. What is photosynthesis? It is the synthesis of sunlight and plant. This symbiosis promotes plant-growth and development. Can we consider teachers as sun rays and students as plants and classroom experiences soil for germination and fruition?

A baby admitted to school imports home everyday some behavioural changes. The tiny tots not only render nursery rhymes and multiplication tables but also show incredible patience and common sense. Perhaps the teacher might have asked the children to examine a flower and count the petals; pick out shells and pebbles from a handful of sand on the sea-shore; plant saplings in the garden, water every day and watch them grow and grow. Each activity transforms a child- to be observant than casual; to be patient than hurried; to be industrious than lazy; to be interdependent than selfish! Parents are perplexed at these behavioural changes and approach the teacher to enquire what magic wand she wielded to effect such a transformation.

What does the teacher reply? She politely says: I just allow them to be themselves. They learn everything by doing what they enjoy doing. They ask many questions. I have no answer for many. Even if I have, I resist my temptation to answer immediately. I do not have a laboratory. The school-garden and field-trips to nearby places are my natural laboratories. I take them out every now and then. They enjoy the freedom and fresh air. I do not load their tiny heads with a cartload of information. It is not needed at all. I assist them to acquire knowledge at their own pace. I do not grade them or compare them. Who am I to tamper with the creations of God! Each child has a potential and it would sprout spontaneously.

Information is not synonymous with education. Real education must transform the learner. When a child feels genuinely sad at the plight of bullocks overburdened with a heavy load on his way to school or when he saves a wounded dog from being run over by a speeding lorry, or when he lends a helping hand to guide the blind person groping in a crowded street, he shows compassion. The transformation in class makes him compassionate. A teacher does not need a computer lab to teach this elementary education. What he needs is genuine concern to transform and not just to inform a child!

"As long as there are postmen, life will have zest."

— *William James.*

"A critic is a man who knows the way but can't drive the car."

—*Kenneth Tynan.*

10

Enhancing the Learner Interest

Recently I attended a lecture on "Teaching strategies" by a retired professor who began with these axioms:

> If you enjoy teaching, students enjoy learning;
> If you endure teaching, students endure learning;
> What is enjoyed endures;
> What is endured does not endure!

This made me recall the delectable feeling I had in many a class when my teacher would transport the students to the very setting in Paris that spurred the imagination of Charles Dickens to write his famous novel, "A Tale of Two Cities" or to the very churchyard that made Thomas Gray pen his immortal poem: "Elegy written in a Country Churchyard"!

Upon reflection I came to realise that a motivated teacher can very much enhance the learning interests and capability of even average learners. Watch a musician enthralling the listeners with some of the subtle nuances of the "raga" with closed eyes and intense ecstasy. He gets lost in the unfathomable ocean of carnatic music. He enjoys his music and thus enables the listeners to join him in the enjoyment.

He might, at times, even be oblivious of the audience. He is applauded for his virtuosity as well as the vitality he brings into his performance. He might be rendering a familiar 'kriti' in a well-known 'raga', but he would embellish the same with amazing creativity, using his 'manodharma'. Why shouldn't a teacher emulate a musician and relish to his heart's content the content of the discipline he handles?

Quite often teachers are apt to find it monotonous and insipid to teach the same subject year after year. This feeling of exhaustion or apathy would rob the very thrill and excitement of presentation. Is there a way out? The only way to overcome this feeling of boredom is to read reference books and journals so as to gain new insight and meaning in the subject. How can a person call himself an experienced teacher unless he really did undergo new experiences in his chosen field? The speaker gave an interesting statement in this regard:

> Experience equals the capacity to teach,
> multiplied by the desire to teach,
> multiplied by the years of service.
> A zero somewhere in that equation
> gives one consequential results.

I realised how hollow it sounds when a teacher boasts of his twenty years of experience when he merely repeats year after year what he taught in the first year. A teacher is not a tape-recorder! Whatever knowledge he gathers is processed by his thinking and imagination. This information-processing model is unique in every teacher. Thus, it gets transformed and delivered in a richer, broader perspective. We find this phenomenon in an abundant measure when a musician elaborates a 'raga' or 'Swaraprastaa' in a new creative manner. Quite often the very occasion of rendering a concert before an appreciative audience would enthuse and energise the performer to weave new contours that he might never have envisaged earlier. There is total involvement. In other words, a teacher should not remain a tape-recorder.

Nothing prevents a teacher from emulating an inspired musician in the art of teaching. Whether one teaches science or mathematics, English or History, one could always heighten and brighten the subject and thus kindle the interest of students. There is nothing like half-hearted performance. Can anyone be alive with half a heart. Similarly, it would be a dead class if a teacher were to be listless in class and teach rather perfunctorily.

There should be an expiry-date for the degree earned in graduation similar to the expiry-date found in a torch-cell. Unless the cell is recharged it is useless. Similarly a teacher needs to constantly replenish and renew knowledge so as to check obsolescence. Only a burning candle can light other candles. Refresher courses are meant to gain new insights, not for passive participation, away from teaching assignments.

A musician has to remain loyal to the tradition and not hobnob with eccentric innovativeness or make incursions into a new school of music. Hybridisation may be counter-productive. "Jugalbandhi" is not so relished as pure carnatic music or Hindustani classical style. A teacher has to be discriminative and discreet in the choice of reading material. He cannot afford to fritter away his energy by reading all kinds of paperbacks that publish untested assumptions and half-truths. It is good to remember the oft-quoted statement of G.K. Chesterton:

> "There is a great deal of difference
> between the eager man who wants
> to read a book and the tired man
> who wants a book to read."

A teacher never gets tired of teaching even after retirment. Perhaps he would enjoy teaching all the more after superannuation.

"Your can discover more about a person in an hour of play than in a year of conversation."

—Plato"

"Gossip is that no one claims to like- but everybody enjoys."

—Joseph Conard.

"Golf is an expensive way of playing marbles"

— *G.K. Chesterton.*

11

Want a Book to Read or to Read a Book?

Most of us read. We read newspapers to keep abreast of the events happening around. We read a magazine to know a little more of the scandals and issues rocking the country. At times we read a refreshing Editorial that condemns flagrant violation of human rights or a palpable injustice meted out to hapless citizens. We are so conditioned to reading the newspaper during morning hours that we get visibly irritated when the paper-boy fails to deliver it on time.

We choose afternoons to read a novel or bed-time to continue the same during a train-journey to complete it. Such readings are relaxed, unhurried and a little casual too. We may have a home library in which we may preserve books that we love to read. However, while waiting in a hair-dressing saloon or a dental clinic we read some old magazines-more to break the monotony than to derive pleasure or profit. The great essayist, G.K. Chesterton said:

> "There is a great deal of difference
> between the eager man who wants to
> read a book and the tired man who
> wants a book to read."

No wonder then that reading occupies primacy in the acquisition of the three R's.

We are taught to read so that we might learn to study. Apparently the two activities look the same. In reality these differ considerably. We study constitutional law, or Newton's Laws of Motion or Mendelian Laws of Heredity or the Law of Diminishing Returns. "Principia Mathematica" is not a novel. It is a book that one needs to study. The author of a book bestows greater attention, care and discrimination in the choice of words to avoid ambiguity. He cannot afford to meander in a labyrinthine style.

Precision, brevity and diction characterise a book which invariably passes through several drafts before print. It is meant to last longer than a magazine or a newspaper. It should not be read casually but studied carefully with a definite purpose, namely to understand, assimilate, store and retrieve at the appropriate time. For example, during school days, one would have learnt to spell the words 'believe' and 'deceive' differently though phonetically these sound similar. One would have referred the dictionary countless times to correct the spelling. This is a deliberate, purposeful and disciplined method.

At times, while reading the centre-page article in the newspaper by the learned jurist V.R. Krishna Iyer, we are forced to have the dictionary within reach to 'learn' the meaning of many unfamiliar words. Still we would remain strangers to such words in future if it is not reinforced again and again.

At school we are taught to study earnestly, diligently and purposefully. We need to bestow sustained attention and interest and shut out all distractions. We undergo this rigorous training so as to remember what we want to remember. We need to learn to forget what we need not remember. It is not possible to remember the total runs of Sachin Tendulkar in every test he played, but the highest individual score of Bradman or Brian Lara are remembered. Kapil Dev's record of wickets in Test Cricket is also remembered. Because, these statistics are repeatedly cited and hence reinforced. Therefore, whatever one needs to remember and recall must be repeated and rehearsed. This is what a text-book writer does.

There is no use in simply reading the definition of Osmosis as "the passing of liquid from a place of high concentration to a place of low concentration through a semipermeable membrane". One must understand what one reads. Blind memorization is called "rote learning". It has poor hold on memory.

Some writers are gifted with the ability to use the apt words to create a vivid imagery that would last long.

For instance, N.A. Palkhivala could not digest the expression, "Committed Judiciary" and he felt it to be a futile attempt to connect North Pole and South Pole. He said, "I cannot imagine a committed `judiciary inasmuch as I cannot imagine a boiling ice-cream!"

Poets are more gifted in this regard. One would love to read Thomas Gray's memorable stanza in "Elegy written in a country churchyard":

"Full many a gem of purest ray serene
The dark unfathom'd caves of ocean bear
Full many a flower is born to blush unseen
And waste its sweetness on the desert air"

I could recite it any time though I read this poem more than half-a-century ago! I possess it almost like my inherited property. If only teachers were to implant in tender minds the zest for study and circumspection in the choice of reading material and also the habit of reciting just for the pleasure of it, what a marvellous miracle it would bring in their lives!

Those who had the pleasure of reading "A Tale of Two Cities" by Charles Dickens would have studied the opening paragraphs countless times"

"It was the age of wisdom,
it was the age of foolishness;
It was the epoch of belief,
it was the epoch of incredulity;
It was the season of light,
it was the season of darkness;
It was the spring of hope,
it was the winter of despair;..."

One could very well sense the intensity of ecstasy the author would have experienced while penning these lines! How can one forget these words!

In good old days, students would shiver entering the class without memorising a poem-a sonnet such as "Daffodils" or "Solitary Reaper" or the definition of important concepts in chemistry or physics. Oral testing was an integral part of classroom teaching. Our teachers were pretty demanding and uncompromising. The defaulters would be put to shame in class. Classroom learning was more serious, individualised and disciplined. That is the reason why the elder citizens today can recite easily the lines from "Kumara Sambhava" or "Raghuvamsa". Sanskrit pandits rarely needed a textbook. They could reel off every line with ease from their prodigious memory.

Memorizing is not an instant affair, but a longitudinal one, gained out of disciplined study. One reads, understands, reads again, reviews, recites, rehearses severals times so that these do not get easily erased. Such a stabilisation results in consolidation. Minimal reading, superficial interest and an indiscreet reliance on an esoteric inspiration would result in forgetting. Modern students tend to sneer at memorizing as if it is an artefact of bygone days! They believe in a robust common sense and reasoning than systematic disciplined memorization while teachers of yore believed in the dictum: "One has to be steady in study" Even non-detailed study of "Gulliver's, Travels" or 'Sindbad the Sailor" or "The Three Musketeers" were read more actively even though these were meant to build one's passive vocabulary.

It is a myth to believe in the atrophy of memory with advancing age. Never does it decline so long as one remained committed and observant. The overconfidence and pseudo-smartness one develops might prompt an individual to slacken the effort to study. Basically, there is a place for relaxed reading and also a place for disciplined study and one needs to know what to do when!

> "Education makes a greater difference between man and man than nature has made between man and brute."
>
> —*John Adams.*

12

Is Punishment Taboo in Schools?

Opinions have been divided among teachers regarding the use of punishment in classrooms. There would always be occasions wherein some students would play mischief and test the patience of teachers. It would not only affect the mood of a teacher adversely but disturb the learning climate of the conscientious section of students. A teacher would be faced with a dilemma-to punish or not to punish.

What kind of punishment would mend the ways of a mischievous or rebellious student is a million dollar question. Of late, teachers are cautious enough to desist from precipitating matters and inviting the wrath of students, parents as well as the Head of the Institution. They endeavour to defuse the situation and strive to maintain a reasonably calm atmosphere in classroom. Yet, on some occasions a teacher would blow his top. Most teachers are human enough to be susceptible to such emotional outbursts, while some are humane enough to understand the root cause of misdemeanours and deal with it appropriately.

After all, every teacher is interested in transforming the crude and rude behaviour of a student into civilised, polished behaviour. As a matter of fact, this is one of the cardinal principles of education. We need to assume that no student is basically bad to deserve severe punishment. Home-background, peer-group influence, unfavourable movies and community life might instigate some to get a thrill in classrooms by becoming notorious rather than famous. By inflicting punishment a teacher would only be worsening the situation rather than ameliorating it. Even though a mischievous student is pretty well aware that he is at fault he does not brook insult in the eyes of his fellow-students. He might go to any extent to settle scores and retaliate outside the school premises. Moreover, the very act of punishment leaves a teacher in a state of diseqilibrium and this might spoil the smooth presentation of lesson. He might suspend the class or teach without zest or go to pieces for the misbehaviour of a few.

If the ultimate objective of education and schooling is something positive and constructive, a teacher needs to ponder and devise a mechanism whereby a student turns over a new leaf. The writer recalls an advice given by an eminent bureaucrat as well as an eminent writer in Tamil. Being invited to address a group of teacher-trainees in a college of Education some four decades ago, the speaker recalled an episode of his school-days. He narrated the incident and allowed the students to draw their own lessons.

This is what he said:

Way back in the thirties, a teacher, renowned for his great compassion to students, had to face a crisis. While everyone had done the assigned homework there was a solitary student who had neither done his homework nor regretted his dereliction of duty. He remained stubborn and asserted his right to disobey. Unmoved by the inexplicable conduct of the boy, the teacher was more than tolerant and volunteered to help him learn to work out the sums if he did not know how to solve them.

The student retorted that he chose not to do homework even though he was capable of doing it. Evidently, the boy was trying to ape a villain in a novel or movie. The poor teacher became a sacrificial goat right in his class. He asked the boy to go to the headmaster's room and fetch a cane. The boy brought it in no time. When he was about to go back to his seat, the teacher requested him to stay on by his side and addressed the class.

"I have always tried to teach as best as I can, and help those who are slow to understand by bestowing special individual attention. I have never disliked any of my students nor has anyone hated me. I am now facing a dilemma. I think I have failed in my mission. In the case of this boy, I have failed and it is but natural that one who has failed needs punishment. I, therefore, ask this student to cane me for my failure to make him learn."

On hearing this, the boy's face turned pale. His arrogance, foolhardiness and pride gave way to tears and repentance. He begged for forgiveness. But, the teacher remained firm and unmoved. He insisted upon being caned. With great reluctance, the boy received the cane from the teacher and gently touched the palm of the teacher's hand with the tip of the cane. Then, he broke down and fell flat upon the feeet of his teacher and begged for pardon. The teacher lifted the boy and hugged him and shed tears of joy. Actually the tip of the cane touched the heart of the boy rather than the palm of the teacher. He turned over a new leaf and turned out to be most outstanding student in the school. Neither did he forget his teacher, nor did the teacher forget him. Punishment, in essence, should be reformative and not retributive. In which case, it is not a taboo at all.

13

Are Rewards Really Catalysts for Better Performance?

Long ago, psychologists like Pavlov, Skinner and Thorndike demonstrated through experiments on animals that rewards act as reinforcing agents to accelerate the learning process and also to enjoy the activity. This generalization has percolated into every classroom. Teachers liberally use marks, grades and other incentives to encourage children to perform better.

Almost every textbook in Psychology quote the experiments of Hurlock on reward and punishment and the effects they have on human motivation. But, recent studies seem to question this assumption. Theresa Amabile, Associate Professor of Psychology, Brandies University, USA, recently published a paper that disproved this theory. She conducted experiments on elementary school and college students and arrived at the conclusion that "rewards can lower performance-levels". A related series of studies showed that "intrinsic interest in a job - the sense that something is worth doing for its own sake - declined when someone was rewarded for doing it."

Neither Pavlov nor Skinner are alive today to lock horns with this researcher! Are we not as teachers, deliberately making children addicts to rewards for performing a learning task that should, as a matter of fact, really excite them and absorb them? Let us say, a Primary class teacher rewards those who never arrive late to school, who always write neatly and legibly and who dress themselves smartly. Fair enough. But, is it a kind of bait offered to children, who should or ought to cultivate this wholesome habit spontaneously and whole-heartedly? Why should they be rewarded at all?

At the high school level there is a scramble for ranks and grades; to score the highest marks in Science and Mathematics particularly. What kind of a pedagogy is it? Neither Marie Curie nor Albert Einstein seem to have been obsessed with such inducements. Yet, they turned out to be outstanding scientists! Even after receiving the Nobel Prize, Marie Curie remained simple. She could not even go to Stockholm to receive the Nobel Prize as she was ill. Scientific temper cannot be sharpened and honed by rewards and punishments!

The whole world eulogises the legendary writer R.K. Narayan for his sparkling humour and his cartoonist brother, R.K. Laxman, for his thoughtful caricature of political heavyweights! We are not sure, whether the former wrote his "Bachelor of Arts" or his "Malgudi Days" with the sole aim of amassing fame and fortune! R.K. Laxman took to cartooning primarily to amuse himself and incidentally to entertain others. We do not know whether his teacher at school would have rewarded him for this talent. Who knows, he might have even received rebukes and retribution for his pranks! However, both the brothers earned a name for themselves in their respective spheres of activity. Did Ramanujan expect bouquet and bonanza from his teachers for his incredible mathematical calculations? Are we then challenging the Behaviourist Skinner's assumption that, "any activity is more likely to occur if it is rewarded"? Kenneth

McGraw, Associate Professor of Psychology at the University of Mississippi cautions that this does not mean Behaviouirsm has been invalidated.

The basic principles of reinforcement and reward certainly work, but in a restricted context; restricted to tasks that are not interesting. Researchers offer several explanations for their surprising findings about rewards and performance. First of all, rewards encourage people to focus narrowly on a task, to do it as quickly as possible and to take few risks. Secondly, people come to see themselves as being controlled by the reward. They feel less autonomous and this may interfere with performance. Finally extrinsic rewards can erode intrinsic interest. People who see themselves as working for money, approval or competitive success find their tasks less pleasurable and therefore, do not do them as well. If we come to view ourselves as working to get something, we will no longer find that activity worth doing in its own right.

In a 1982 study, Stanford Psychology Professor, Mark L. Lepper showed that any task, no matter how enjoyable it seemed, would be devalued if it were presented as a means rather than an end. He told a group of pre-schoolers they could not engage in one activity they liked until they first took part in another. Although they had enjoyed both activities equally, the children came to dislike the task that was a prerequisite for the other. In a study of corporate employees, Ryan found that those who were told, "Good, you're doing as you should," were significantly less intrinscially motivated than those who were not told so.

High school students evince an insatiable urge to read books and novels of their choice such as the works of Victor Hugo, Jonathan Swift and of course, the invincible Enid Blyton! But, they are not allowed to indulge in this kind of pleasurable reading as their teachers would have given them an assigment on the prescribed text. Under duress they submit an assignment on the "Voyage of Marco Polo" or "The rise and fall of Vijayanagar Empire", merely to be in the good books of teachers and parents. Perhaps, at a later day they would read the same material with renewed zest because no one compelled them to study the book.

Quite naturally students would look forward to the day of emancipation from these rewards so that they can reward themselves by doing what they really wanted to do. Teachers and parents alike must keep it in mind that rewards need not always necessarily mean a road to better performance.

"Have the courage to take your own thoughts seriously for they will shape you"

— *Einstein.*

"I do not like to commit myself about heaven and hell- you see, I have friends in both places."

— *Mark Twain.*

"Everything should be made as simple as possible, but not simpler."

— *Einstein.*

"Silence is the unbearable repartee"

— *G.K. Chesterton.*

14

For Whom the Bell Rings?

Babies can be consoled, cajoled, cheered and activated by ringing a bell. The sound of a bell triggers a spontaneous urge to crawl and get hold of the bell. Even during the preschool stage the bell continues to be an object of pleasure and excitement. Its resonance seems to vibrate the sensitive chords of the ears and afford joy.

Tiny tots say "Ta Ta" to their parents as they leave for school in the morning with shining shoes and well-pressed, uniforms. To these tiny creatures, schooling is a kind of jolly outing from the confines of a home. They would board the school bus, play with their friends, watch the shops and buildings "en route", welcome their friends who board at intermediate points and be on time at school to join the morning assembly.

At the sound of the bell children march in a line to the open ground and stand in a row for invocation and sermon. They could be conditioned to be in attention or stand_at_ease by a bell or whistle and also to remain quiet or squat (if the sermon is rather long) and to disperse in an orderly way at the end.

As soon as they reach their classrooms, their boisterousness surfaces and they seem to enjoy the pandemonium. The bell rings again, producing a kind of unbelievable silence! The teacher is sighted and the routine gets under way. Teaching-learning process follows. We don't have to bother much about the kind of teaching and the kind of learning! Minutes crawl.

Between the exit of a teacher and the arrival of another, children could activate their vocal chords to the maximum. In other words, they are back to their instincts. Another spell of teaching-learning exercise follows. It could be a monologue or a dialogue. Kids have admirable adaptability to both situations. Bell rings and everyone heaves a sigh of relief!

As the sun moves toward the West and the shadows fall in full length, children prepare themselves for their freedom from bondage. Of course, teachers too look forward to their deliverance. A long bell rings and all, who long for it know for sure what it means. Scramble for seats in the school bus starts and pretty soon kids, get back to their homes as the clock chimes five.

15

Students Must have Clear Priorities

A random survey among college students would reveal the startling finding of aimlessness. A vast majority are blissfully unaware of what they want to be in life. They just drift like a rudderless boat. It is like boarding any train in a junction not knowing clearly one's destination. Precious time, youth and money get drained.

As one crosses the middle stage of schooling one has to be at least dimly aware of the direction of his life. A good many grope in the dark. In subtle ways teachers of all subjects could shed some light upon the vocational avenues of the school disciplines. These are days of specialisation. Generalised education does not lead us anywhere.

Are parents in a position to guide their wards? Only a few are wise in this regard. Quite unwittingly some do harm than good. They are guided by societal expectations and monetary compensations rather than their potential. By endeavouring to live upto the pious hopes and lofty expectations of parents, many youngsters would be in a quandary mainstream.

Here is a profile of a goal-directed student. Mr. X was an above average student at school. He had an admiration for his teachers. They were not only proficient in the subjects they taught, but were also humane and helpful. He could notice sparkle in their eyes while teaching. Evidently they enjoyed teaching. Mr. X nursed a desire to become a teacher. Soon after graduation Mr. X chose to join a college of education despite his parents' suggestion that he would have brighter prospects in Banking services. But Mr. X remained firm in his resolve to be a teacher. He did become a teacher. He never took his students for granted. Rather, he felt they were granted to him. Never did he go to his class unprepared. He was conscious of his responsibility of moulding and shaping the lives of his students. He had a sense of fulfilment. His earnings were moderate. But, he earned the goodwill of his pupils in an abundant measure. His students were motivated to learn from a motivated teacher."

The foregoing description is a hypothetical case of a committed, conscientious teacher. An analysis would reveal the following characteristics:

(i) Goal-directed behaviour.

(ii) Emulation of worthy models

(iii) Sustained interest crystallised into a definite vocation.

(iv) A sense of fulfilment - job satisfaction

(v) Realistic level of aspiration

(vi) Self-actualisation.

Everyone has to have an "aim" or "goal" in life. It has a personal frame of reference. No two individuals need necessarily have an identical goal. The goal an individual sets for oneself should be "attainable" and "meaningful". In this process one is guided by one's "Self-concept". It is an accurate realistic perception of one's potentialities as well as shortcomings. This awareness alone would help an individual set such a goal that would be in harmony with the true "self".

Such an individual would not be vacillating and enticed by the allurements of alternative goals. One would neither consider himself/herself lower or higher than his fellow human beings who have different goals. Since the goal one has chosen has a personal significance it is likely to 'energise' and 'motivate' an individual a great deal. Upon attaining such a goal one tends to experience "fulfilment" and satisfaction. From the mental health point of view, such motivated individuals are likely to contribute a lot for societal well-being. In the case of the illustration cited above, Mr. X had a clear-out goal in life even as a student at school. Naturally, his motivation in the chosen vocation must be of a high order.

Every individual has goals and he aspires to achieve this goal. In the course of achieving this goal he has some "expectations". The standard he wants to achieve in any task is described by psychologists as his "Level of Aspiration". It is closely related to his "self-esteem".

Motivation and aspiration affect each other in their actual functioning. The young child has to be guided and helped in the process of setting a level of aspiration appropriate for him. Setting too high a goal beyond the potential abilities of an individual will have disturbing effects, providing a sense of frustration, which may competely disorganise the energy-system.

Such experiences bring in negative reactions like feelings of inferiority or aggression. Level of aspiration should be high enough to be challenging and low enough to be attainable. It reflects one's peraonality. It is related to one's self-concept.

16

Avoid Evaluation that Generates Tension

Anxiety is a silent killer. It can cripple your capacity, freeze your effort and paralyse your personality. Yet, it is commonly experienced, or rather tolerated. Life is full of testing times. From the kindergarten stage till you breathe your last, anxiety pervades everyone in every activity. We are not born with it. It is cultivated.

Quite unwittingly parents foster anxiety in kids. By nature, kids enjoy mingling with other kids or would even enjoy playing with their teachers. Teachers showering kindness could make kids feel at home in school. It should be an instinct in a teacher and not an artificial exterior.

There is no place for anxiety in an atmosphere of freedom, acceptance and appreciation. Why do we then make infinite efforts to generate anxiety among children? Parents are anxious to see that their kids obtain a good grade. What a degrading practice to grade kids in their ability to recite letters of the alphabet, days of the week or months of the year. Take this episode as an example for a situational analysis of different behaviours.

"Are you a boy or a girl, Smitha?" The teacher asks an upper KG. student. Smitha looks puzzled. She does not give a straight answer. She is confused. She replies, "Why, Madam, Don't I look like a girl? Do I look like a boy? Are you teasing me? I am always a girl? I will never be a boy in this birth." What a spontaneous, creative answer!

But, this is not something that her teacher expected. Supposing the teacher were to ask the same question to Sowmya, she would stand up and say clearly, "I am a girl."

To this kind of reply, the teacher would say, "Very good. Sit down." At the end of the year, taking note of the subject marks and observing their behaviour, every student is graded for academic studies and general behaviour in school. In the light of this, how would Sowmya be graded?..... What would be Smitha's fate? - Talkative Impertinent, proud! After all Smitha was reacting to a silly question in an intelligent manner. She was least anxious. She was just her natural self. But, Smitha is shocked when her teacher reacted, "Smitha, Don't act smart. Be polite. All that I wanted was a straight answer. Why do you give a lecture? Be a good girl.

Smitha is hurt. She apologises for no reason. "No madam. I just spoke what I felt. I never meant offence. I did not know why you asked this question. Am I at fault? Please don't report this to my mummy. She would scold me. Henceforth I would say just this much, "I am a girl."

If I were to be her teacher I would give her the following grade: "E" - Excellent. An exceptionally bright and lively kid; Capable of developing into an extroverted, intelligent girl. Does not feel anxious at all in a test-situation.

Anxiety gets accelerated in a test-situation. Because, a test is always tagged on to a reward-punishment system. It is a test of memory-power. You have to answer within a time-frame. The atmosphere is tense. You are watched, and supervised. You receive your answer paper with a grade or mark. Such competitions could be heartening or disheartening. You are always compared and ranked, because that is the way we have been brought up. You are always expected to be ahead of your class-mates. You and Lakshmi might be good friends. But, the friendship would develop fissures the moment she is ranked higher and you are at a lower level. Lakshmi looks triumphant.

You look defeated and hence despondent. Feelings of anxiety swell when you take the next test. As kids, naturally we are not mentally nature enough to take it otherwise. You avoid the company of Lakshmi. You remain secretive. All these are daily experiences of kids.

It is within our powers to rid kids of anxiety. Divide children into smaller groups. Assign each group with varied activities. Do not encourage group-rivalry. Ask five kids to pluck leaves from the school garden and examine minutely the parts of the leaves. Ask another five kids to pluck flowers from different plants. Ask them to report what they observed. Ask another five kids to examine to bark or trunk of different trees. Let them report. Another five could be encouraged to compose a small poem on trees and plants.

When each group makes a presentation in class, it would be thrilling to listen to several aspects being spoken, rather than getting tensed and being compared 'for grades'. Such presentations could be recorded and sent to parents.

When you free a child from the anxiety of taking a test and also avoid the kind of evaluation that might generate tension and suspicion, education can certainly be an enlivening experience. By implanting anxiety in a test or a comparative grading situation, all the time comparing one another, you are a actually robbing the children of the zest for learning.

17

Setting a Question Paper

Of all the irksome, yet unavoidable duties of the profession of Teaching, setting an ideal question paper continues to remain the weakest link. Many yearn for this dubious honour, but most, when offered choose to remain indifferent, if not, indolent. Normally, more than adequate time for preparation is given by concerned authorities, hoping piously for, a well-designed comprehensive question paper. Alas! What a disappointment! Teachers who never fail to preach students in classrooms, "Procrastination is the thief of time", have absolutely no qualms of conscience to abrogate this dictum. Days roll by and even the deadline is crossed. Reminders are sent to rush the question paper as the examination is fast approaching. Quite a few choose to ignore even this reminder-call. Another reminder is sent. Then alone, the learned teacher is aroused like "Rip Van Winkle." Glancing at the Contents of the syllabus quickly and surveying the question papers of previous years carefully, a question paper is prepared rather haphazardly. All the precautions like adequate coverage of the syllabus, appropriate structuring of questions, judicious mix of easy, difficult and moderate types of questions so as to cater to the needs of the dull, gifted and above average learners, due weightage for each question and optimum time-limit for answering- all such healthy parameters are abandoned. Somehow the job must be completed and forgotten. The sanctity of secrecy associated with this sacred trust is violated with impunity with the result leakage of question papers hardly raises a flutter. This is the stark reality. The paper-setter would rationalise thus: "After all, what they pay for setting a question paper is just a pittance. Why should I strain? This much would suffice for this much remuneration". The festering wound would never heal so long we have such lotus-eaters and left-overs in the profession of teaching once adorned by lofty individuals! Teaching has ceased to be the sacred mission that it once was. The flood-gates are thrown open to allow all and sundry. Thus quality has become the casualty. In bygone days teaching remained the prerogative of the principled preceptors. They were not mercenaries or mendicants.

They would prepare meticulously for each class, regardless of their years of experience in teaching. They would have framed a number of developmental questions while planning each lesson. Such questions would dawn only in the minds of those teachers who really loved teaching. Some of the thought-provoking questions raised by bright students in class would also be included in this Question-Bank! Therefore, setting a question paper would not pose a problem to them. They would pull out of the Question-Bank a good number of intelligent questions so as to prepae a comprehensive question-paper.

Unless a teacher cultivates such a healthy habit of planning a lesson and framing developmental questions, he cannot set an ideal question-paper. One has to prepare a blueprint. Some questions have to be of the recall-type. Some will have to be at the understanding-level. Some must generate original thinking. The proportion of each type must correspond to the learner-capability of students. Weightage has to be judiciously provided for each category. Challenging questions can be answered only by the bright. Therefore, such questions have to be very few. Since the majority of students belong to the mediocre level of achievement such questions will have to outnumber difficult questions.

However, each question must make students think. Examination should not remain a mere memory-test. Questions should not be ambiguous. Vauge questions would elicit vague answers. The entire syllabus should be covered. Short-answer questions are preferable to long essay questions. Students must feel happy they were given an opportunity to reveal their knowledge. They should not feel they were outwitted by unexpected and unanswerable questions. Examination-reform is needed to make it fair, transparent and student-friendly. Moderation of question-paper is absolutely necessary so that ugly demonstration by aggrieved students is averted.

In short, question-paper setting is not an instant affair. In a way it is a test of a teacher's sustained, consistent effort to provide quality education all through the academic year.

> "It was very good of God to let Carlyle and Mrs. Carlyle marry each other and so make only two people miserable instead of four."
>
> — *Samuel Butler.*

18

The Pernicious Fall-out of Ranking

The much awaited examination results are out, bringing cheer to a few and gloom to the vast multitude. One could perceive the beaming smiles of the "rankers", the bleeding eyes of the "less-fortunates", not to speak of the despondency of those left far behind. Quite unusually we find many parents revolting against palpable malpractice in evaluation that caused discrepancy between anticipation and dispensation. The malady is a deeprooted systemic failure.

After ten long years of schooling from standard I every student awaits with bated breath the Day of Judgement. All the fun in schooling, the numerous friendships made, and ever so many memorable reminiscences seem inconsequential when the inexorable examination - results leave a lot of cleavages among students. Have we not inadvertently brainwashed students by blowing out of proportion ranks and grades as the sole yardstick of scholastic performance? Has it not sent shivers upon the spine of parents? Has it not reduced schools to mere coaching shops wherein a relentless grinding replaces rejuvenating teacher-pupil interaction? The excitement of discovery, the exuberance of experimentation, the ecstasy of participation in debates and discussions, and above all, the eagerness to read for fun and enjoyment, seem to be sacrificed at the altar of sharpening one's skill in responding to anticipated questions with tailor-made answers! In this process, creative thinking is decimated, convergent thinking promoted, and pupil-participation eliminated! What remains is the plain filling-in of predigested bits of information into the tiny heads, to be regurgitated in examination-halls!

Schools vie with one another to advertise the rich haul of ranks appropriated by flashing the photographs of the triumphant candidates. Parents of such privileged prodigies swell with pride upon the glory and they are hell-bent on whipping the winning horses so as to sustain the spree for a couple of years more - to secure a safe berth in a professional course ! It gives the students the dubious distinction of becoming eminent scholars whereas in reality they have only demonstrated their prowess to store and retrieve information from their memory-banks!

This is not to deny those "rankers" or "toppers" the credit they deserve for their superlative performance. This is only to underscore the tragedy of their suffering rather than enjoying school-life. Academic achievement is not the "Summum bonum" of education. It is just one segment of Personality-development. We need to take a holistic view of schooling to include a number of auxiliary traits that every student ought to cultivate during their formative years. Activities that should remain ever green in their memories such as conducting an investigatory project, organising an exhibition, participation in games and sports and enjoying music and dramatics are sidelined, if not shut-out. Are we manufacturing human robots or creative individuals?

What about those who missed the ranks by a whisker? Despair and gloom envelope their homes. Parents feel let down because their sons/daughters failed to steal the limelight! Instead of patting them with encouraging comments such as, "Well done!" they are harangued by the refrain, "you should have put in more effort!"

Eminent jurist, Mr. N.A. Palkhivala, in his convocation Address of the Bangalore University on 15th January, 1972 observed:

> "As regards those who have not been as successful in their examinations as they thought they deserved to be I can only recall the words of Prof. Walter Raleigh that the College final and the Day of Judgement are two different examinations. They may also take some consolation from the fact that A.E. Houseman, the great scholar of Greek and Latin and better known as a poet, once failed in the papers on those very languages at the Oxford University. His biographer, Richards comments, "The Nightingale got no prize at the poultry show!"

Should we allow such a lop-sided perception of education to continue? Is it not our duty to stem the rot and make schooling an exciting voyage of discovery rather than a cramming centre? We need to create "knowledge-seekers" and not "book-worms"; children who would venture to make shrewd guesses than safe, correct answers; and the courage to make new pathways rather than traverse beaten-tracks! We need a public debate on this issue of "ranking and grading" to re-wash the brain!

19

Legitimise Copying in Examinations

As March marches out and April dawns every year, it not only shoots up the mercury level but also gives rise to a feverish fervour among students to burn the midnight oil in order to acquit themselves creditably in public examinations which determine their future. The plight of supervisors in the examination-hall is unenviable. It is not uncommon to come across instances of invigilators being subjected to intimidation and humiliation at the hands of hoodlums masquerading as students. Malpractices in examination are not a new phenomenon. It has been there from the hoary past. Only the incidence has increased of late. Once upon a time it used to be a kind of an aberration confined to a few individuals. Now, it is a disease afflicting many.

Copying in the examination hall has become an all-pervasive factor at all levels. Quite a few heads of institutions as well as the faculty members just wink at it, if not connive at it. Does it not make a mockery of all that the students had learnt throughout the year? If one has the nerve, one could always cheat and get away with it. There is no question of morality or sanctity in examinations to deflect their actions since all ethical values are decimated by their own mentors. It is high time, therefore, that educationists came to grips with the malady and legitimised copying, if they cannot eliminate it. Neither moralising nor policing is going to bring the desired results.

As preceptors it is our paramount duty to transmit knowledge and wisdom to those who seek. But, does everyone seek knowledge? Among those students present in any class, there could be a handful of dedicated ones. Some approach their studies spontaneously, prompted by an intrinsic motivation to learn and grow. Some are motivated to procure a degree that guarantees an opening in the employment market. Some are pushed and prodded by parents to join an institution, not exactly knowing why they are there. In other words, they just drift. The majority of "Copy writers" belong to the third category. They are immune to any kind of healthy attitudes and interests. They would not suffer compunction in these matters. There is no use in preaching altruistic values to them.

Since public examinations have become an obsession with the vast majority of students, and since procrastination has become an accepted pattern of behaviour with them, the copying business has come to stay. Some students are habituated to it from their school days and cannot outgrow the habit. Examinations must be passed through fair means or foul. The end at last justifies the means for them.

How do we arrest this menace? Or, do we have to arrest it at all? What are the options? We could offer instruction in a cluster of subjects and give students an opportunity to benefit from the same. We need not go through the travails of conducting an examination at the end of it, especially an examination which encourages malpractices. After all, most employment agencies have designed their own entrance tests. Malpractice of any kind would be ruthlessly put down in these centres. No surreptitious practices would be permissible.

Why not give a fair trial to this novel scheme and close down the examination-wing in universities and other boards? These places have become dens of corruption.

The second option is to conduct a series of tests all through the year/semester, wherein the quantum of subject-content would be limited. The panic and tension also would be very much reduced. Students could be made aware of their progression or stagnation, and corrective action could be taken, if necessary. If tests are designed in a semi-objective way, they would lend themselves for fair assessment with the help of a key. There would be no room for corruption or heart-burning among students. Five or six tests spread over the academic term could be allotted 80 per cent weightage, leaving just 20 percent for the final comprehensive examination. Sceptics may throw this suggestion overboard, doubting the integrity of the teaching faculty. However, it is a tragedy that students sit and listen to lectures, take down notes religiously and even seek clarification. But, they do not trust their evaluation, because there are always a few black sheep in the teaching community. They should be spotted, charge-sheeted and dismissed outright. We should not allow these cancerous cells to grow and multiply. The surgery is long overdue!

The third alternative is to legitimise copying. It may sound paradoxical. Actually it has been in vogue in many universities in other countries. What is legitimate copying? Allow students to bring any book or notes to the examination-hall. Let them refer as often as they wish. Frame questions in such a way that unless one has read through the text and supplementary materials, one would never be in a position to locate the answers. This is called "Open-Book Examination", which has successfully been practised elsewhere. Such an examination would easily distinguish the earnest student from the lotus eaters. One could give 50 per cent or even more weightage to the final examination. Invigilation would become less hazardous in this system.

As long as student-achievement is evaluated only in one final examination, which involves the setting of a question-paper, evaluation of stereotyped answers, tabulation of marks followed by the announcement of dubious result-everything that is done with a lot of unnecessary paraphernalia, added to doubtful secrecy-students would be inclined to cheat. It would not be a bad idea to get representatives of students from several colleges for a face-to-face discussion with the University authorities and senior faculty numbers to evolve a consensus in this matter which would be acceptable to all. After all, colleges and universities are not meant to make them captives to a system that has outlived its use.

> "Twenty million young women rose to their feet with the cry "We will not be dictated to" and promptly became stenographers."
>
> — *G.K. Chesterton.*

20

Rank Obsession

Mark Twain observed, "I never let schooling to interfere with my education." It is relevant even to-day. During ancient times parents remained educators. Youngsters acquired knowledge and wisdom partly by emulation and partly by instruction. Values and education formed a symbiotic synthesis. In a family everyone acquired what he/she was capable of doing. There was no necessity of comparison or competition. Some took to agriculture and acquired a lot of knowledge regarding crops, animal husbandry, storage of grain, selling and so on. Some became proficient in music or dance and learnt the nuances with diligence and love. Some learnt Vedic hymns and perpetuated the family tradition. Some chose to acquire formal learning in an institution so as to prepare oneself for a vocation. Each one differed in his pursuits and seldom had he any occasion to run a race against another. There was harmony in the family, peace in the village and prosperity in society.

What a transformation have we brought about in our modern dynamic society! We use high-sounding terms like Information Technology, Software programming, Human Resources Management, Bio-technology, Global warming, Ozone Depletion, Artificial Intelligence, Gender Equality so on and so forth. The list is endless.

Behind all these fancy terms lies the basic human nature and its refinement due to acculturation. God has endowed every creation with certain basic potential that would manifest under appropriate stimulation and encouragement. An education worth the name ought to tap the hidden talents submerged within the "psyche" and nurture so that it might blossom and enliven society.

Let us take literature. We had a Tolstoy, Tagore, Tennyson, Twain, Dickens, Hardy, Milton, Wordsworth, Shakespeare, Eliot, Goldsmith and several hundreds! Did they, in their scholastic days make a feverish attempt to outshine or outsmart their colleagues? Did they not achieve excellence in their own ways and enrich their lives and the lives of others! It is meaningless to compare one another. Wordsworth remained a Solitary Reaper; Hardy was far from the madding Crowd; Shakespeare rejoiced in his midsummer nights' dreams' Pearl Buck loved this Good Earth; Albert Camus witnessed the Plague; Dickens found delight in a Bleak House. How! Why? Each one was individualistic. Each enjoyed his/her idiosyncrasies!

Winston Churchill had a dig at his teachers, and examinations. He said, "They are more interested in-knowing what I do not know than what I do know. While I would have willingly displayed my knowledge they sought to fathom my ignorance. "Decades have rolled by since Churchill made this indignant comment. The situation has never improved; rather it has worsened.

Photographs of promising youngsters- 'toppers' as they are called - are flashed in newspapers. Institutions get publicity - a sort of advertisement to woo the clientele. Are students Derby horses to declare the 'jackpot'? At best these guys have demonstrated their cognitive development in an examination predominantly based on recall of textual material.

It might give the dubious distinction of excellence, but the "summum bonum" of real education spills over these examination-performance.

Has an individual developed his skill in creative writing, Scientific discovery, proficiency in a game or athletic activity, oratory and debates, Fine Arts and a quest for truth? Very few formal institutions seem to foster such traits because many of these do not lend themselves to be graded, ranked and extolled. Ranking can cause a psychological scar on millions of learners while it can intoxicate a few! It might also make many school authorities mistake knowledge for wisdom. Even those few who make it to the top would have gone through a neurotic experience at the heat of examinations. One would have burnt midnight oil, crammed a lot, assimilated little, appreciated nothing in the agony of breasting the winning tape!

It is really sad to note that modern education has to prepare the youngsters for a competitive life. There seems to be no ray of hope on the horizon to emancipate education from examination and competition and "rank-obsession".

> "When Adlai Stevenson was awarded an honorary degree in 1959, he said he found it both tempting and trecherous- "tempting because we all hope to be mistaken for scholars, and bad because if you then make a speech, the mistake is quickly exposed."

21

Parenting

There is a sea-change among parents in contemporary times in child-upbringing. Not that parents of earlier times were callous or non-committal. More importance is attached to foster 'achievement-motivation" and concomitant tension. Rightly or wrongly we have allowed educational institutions of all kinds to mushroom in society that vie with one another in accelerating cognitive development. The patience we observe in permitting a bud to blossom into a flower is seldom practised in moulding and shaping children. Teachers attempt to push into the tiny heads of kids artificial symbolism in the garb of linguistic stills. A minority of children with a genetic advantage manage to survive and remain afloat while a vast majority get drowned in the bottomless sea of education! Unwittingly we contribute to the proliferation of slow-learners or non-learners.

Parents cannot countenance marginalisation of their kids in class. Everytime a baby brings back bad homework that are indiscreetly mutilated by inept teachers, the blood-pressure of parents rises abnormally. Affection is replaced by admonition. Attachment is superseded by impeachment! At an age when kids can hardly understand the value of formal, compulsory education, they are prodded and pushed to perform well. The cognitive hillock is always an ascent, with no prospect of a plateau where one can rest and refresh, enjoy the meadows, roll on the grass, watch squirrels, caterpillars and butterflies!

Rousseau would brand modern parents and teachers culprits under the section, 'Violation of Children's rights'. Are we right in depriving kids of their rights to be wrong in spelling or computing in class and reinforcing in kids an obsessive urge to remain always right? There is no left side at all as far as children are concerned, because teachers and parents are afraid that kids would be left behind if they took the left route!

No honest answer is given to a child who asks why there are only twenty-six letters in the alphabet and who designed or decided the shape of each letter and who coined so many words to fill a bulky dictionary! There is no time to answer such silly questions!

> "Happiness is a butterfly, which, when pursued is always beyond your grasp, but which, if you will sit down quietly, may alight upon you"
>
> —*Nathaniel Hawthorne.*

22

A Mother's Dilemma and Daughter's Response

Long long ago, when I gave birth to my first child, carried the little baby in my arms, caressed her silken hair, fluffy cheeks and tender fingers, little did I foresee that sometime in the far off future will I have to face a dilemma- the uncertainty of rearing a child. After all I brought her up the way I was brought up by my parents. Of course, my parents would pass the buck to their parentage. I am neither an obscurantist nor an ultra-modern one, but would place myself 'in-between'.

Approaching middle-age, with a few silvery hair sneaking here and there, I find it irksome to fall in line with the thinking of my growing sons and daughters. I can't help recapturing the nostalgic memories of their total dependency upon my tender care. I taught them how to speak, count and dress too! But now! They seldom speak to me the way they should speak to a mother. The way they dress is outrageous! My advice is summarily dismissed!

I do not know whether I stimulated or stifled their growth. Have I not granted them more freedom than I myself enjoyed during my childhood and adolescence? You see, this concession is stretched far too long, so much so, you begin to feel you could be dispensed with. How can I allow myself to be taken for granted and dictated to by my own children?

Did I not send them to good schools, piously hoping they would cultivate the elementary etiquettes like courtesy, humility, honesty and responsibility? Of course, they did imbibe a few of these virtues. But, they also picked up a few detestable mannerisms from their peers. I wouldn't blame their teachers for this drift. Quite often their admonition and advice would fall on deaf ears. A bevy of loquacious girls in a class can give hell to a conscientious teacher and drive her out of the class. Often the teacher appeals to the mother to help her in controlling the boisterous girls!

There is an alarming increase of magazines in recent times. I find it necessary to censor even some of the popular ones because the stories, and sketches do not seem to cater to good taste. I wonder how a writer could possibly wield the pen so recklessly, to paint a lurid spectacle of lust and violence. I am facing a dilemma. Should I allow all these stuff to reach my drawing room or shall I boycott them? How could I monitor the movements of my grown-ups all the time? They could always have access to the proscribed literature and keep them surreptitiously beneath their pillows! They derive a peculiar thrill in pursuing a forbidden act, presumably to proclaim their emancipation.

Daughter Replies..........

I read your dilemma with pleasure as well as anguish. I had never imagined that beneath your benign exterior so many sentiments were packed. Believe me, I love you all the more. Do you know, why? I may also become a mother like you sooner or later. I may experience whatever I made you experience. Would you listen to my past with patience?

I do not know where I was born until you pointed to an imposing building one evening on my fifth birthday when we had a stroll. You whispered into my ears that you delivered me on the fifth floor of that maternity hospital. It meant nothing to me then. But now, having studied Biology at school, I guess, you must have struggled to accommodate me within you for about a couple of hundred days! I must have given you a lot of trouble from "within" as I have been pestering you from outside these days! You must have had immense relief after letting me out. I wonder why the Creator had deprived me the memory of my first year, your caressing, kissing and embracing my fluffy cheeks! I do recollect the lovely teddy-bear you presented me on my second birthday, the tricycle on my third and that lovely school-bag on my fourth birth-day. I haven't forgotten my first day at school when you coaxed me to mix with strange kids and a stranger teacher, despite my tearful pleas to take me home.

How nicely would you dress me with a pink frock, tie a red ribbon around my curly hair, put on the cosy canvas shoes upon my tiny feet and say "ta ta" in the morning! How anxiously would you be expecting me in the evening with a "laddu" upon my return from school? I would feel restless at school beyond 3 o'clock'.

You had never spared me the daily ritual of reciting multiplication tables, days of the week, months of the year, and the nursery rhymes too. Do not scold me now when I say I did all these not because I really enjoyed, but I was sure of a sweet if I obeyed you. I remember how you would tighten your grip on my wrist whenever I crossed a busy road and also how often you had denied me cone ice-cream in cinema theatres'. I did not understand why you cried in some movies, nor did you understand why I cried in some movies- when the big elephant was caught in a trap and the spotted deer devoured by the lion. You would wipe off my tears and give me a toffee, but I would cry endlessly.

You had never pardoned me for stealing my brother's crayons and hiding these in my school-bag. Nor did you spare me for losing the lunch-box. I still remember the nice beatings you gave me for my refusal to go to bed when we had guests and also for my reluctance to leave the bed in the morning to get ready for the school. You would sit by me while I was down with fever and allow me to fondle the fluffy doll kept on the show-case. I cannot forget those days! They are gone for ever!

I am now grown up and you can see I am taller than you are. I have more friends. I can run faster than you do. I read a lot. But, I owe you all that I had and will always remember the warmth of your lap on which I had slept many a day! Haven't you observed birds hatching their eggs and watching the young ones breaking open the shells to breathe fresh air? Still the mother-bird would feed the young ones, protect them from cats until these are strong enough to fly and take care of themselves. My feathers have grown and multiplied. I can now hop from branch to branch, fly from tree to tree. I would come back to you when the Sun sets and darkness prevails. I may have to leave you some day. Or, you may have to leave me some day. But, you would always be in my thoughts as I would always be in yours. Will any one be more forgiving in this world than a mother and will anyone be more grateful than a daughter?

23

Liberty and Licence

We have spent the first half of our life listening to the older generation. We spend the second half listening to the younger generation! Life, like a river, always moves in one direction. Never does it take a reverse direction. In retrospect, we have no regrets, nurse no grudges for having lived in accordance with the dictates of elders under whose benevolent patronage we grew up. After all, they were benevolent authorities, not malevolent authoritarians! Never did we question the sanctity of the commandment of our parents and grand parents. In a joint-family system it was considered impolite and insolent to dispute or displease elders. Whatever they prescribed we accepted in good faith unquestioningly, even though at times we felt we were denied our liberty to do what we wanted to do. We realise now that uneducated liberty, is no liberty at all; it is a kind of pseudo-liberty shackled to one', own self-interest! Since the whole society observed such norms none experienced conflicts. Whenever someone violated the code of conduct surreptitiously his conscience pricked and made him feel guilty and repentant. Looking back, we realise, our lives were not wasted! 'Rather, we remain ever grateful to those sagacious elders (who are no more alive) for having disciplined us discreetly at a time when we had no power of discrimination to distinguish the right from the wrong. Such a pattern of living has become anarchronistic nowadays!

Life beyond sixty can be exciting as well as exasperating. One should learn to adapt to reality and take ringside view. Our grandchildren demand freedom far too early in life and get it too! Though we could succeed to some extent in bringing up our children the way we thought it appropriate, our grandchidren seem to be emancipated right from their early childhood. They are pampered and permitted to do whatever they wish to do. Our words of advice fall on deaf ears. We are told that value-system has undergone a sea-change and transformation. We remain mute spectators to the new theories of child-upbringing and child-rearing practices wherein liberty and licence are indistinguishable! Worse still, we are being accused of being tyrannical and authoritarian in our ways of upbringing. We realise that it would be foolhardiness and waste of time to argue with those who refuse to be changed. Looking at some of the glaring instances of misbehaviour of youngsters these days we realise we made no mistakes!

Our grandchildren can get whatever they want whenever they accompany their parents to an exhibition or park or circus. Ice-cream, chocolates, Pepsi, Fanta and what not! would be provided without much bargain. The consequent sickness, absence from school are accepted smugly. "After all, they are kids. If they don't enjoy life now, when will they enjoy?" This is the explanation offered by indulgent parents. Do things happen according to their pious expectations? Having been accustomed to get whatever they demanded, they grow up to be all the more rebellious and unyielding. It might be too late to mend ways because they are not taught to bend in their formative years!

24

When Knowledge Becomes a Burden...

One of the oft-repeated criticisms of school education hovers around the ever-expanding frontiers of curriculum. There seems to be no let-up. Let us not expend our energy upon the hair-splitting semantic distinction between syllabus and curriculum. It would suffice if we, for the present, address ourselves to the burden that kids are saddled with, in terms of textual content and exercises and other auxiliary activities to supplement class-instruction from the 'grass-root' to the 'shoot-level'.

Do these little creatures find time to 'stand and stare', 'relax and reflect' and 'rest on oars'? They seem to be perpetually on the move. They are goaded in class, pressured at home, and they get worked up, in peer-group competition almost breathlessly. They have too much to learn, too little time to digest, almost no time to debate or dispute. It is time we posed the question: Are the schools to blame for this rat-race? Or, are we to blame the overambitious parents who are hell-bent on accelerating the cognitive development of their little ones? Or, do we find fault with society at large for having created an obsession to carry the "Information Technology fever" to the ludicrous limit of making kids a walking encyclopaedia!

It is considered a deficiency syndrome if kids were to confess their ignorance about a few things. One is expected to have a nodding acquaintance of everything under the Sun.

At the stroke of the final school-bell in the evening children rush out of classes with a sigh of relief, to renew their freedom from bondage! Alas! What a shortlived satisfaction! Not being content with what is being "stuffed-in" within the confines of the classroom, `benevolent' parents in their progeny's interest, despatch them once again to tuition classes to supplement if not supplant school-instruction. Most children are goaded to broaden their "intellectual horizon" by attending computer classes that have mushroomed in every nook and corner. Those at the threshold of adolescence attend coaching institutes for professional courses with a view to vying for admission to prestigious institution that would guarantee an exodus to the exotic land of promise!

A systematic brainwashing is done from childhood, to make the children feel ashamed of their land of birth, to uproot them from their native soil and seek asylum in an alien land. How could we ensure this? Feed them more and more at school with a plethora of facts and figures.

A kind of infanticide is taking place insidiously. Many of the healthy hobbies like general reading for pleasure, participation in out-door games, a quiet convivial conversation among friends and relatives, visits to places of worship and cultural entertainments are marginalised. To fulfil the aspirations of parents, school syllabus gets enriched and expanded periodically. At times, poor teachers are compelled to update their content-knowledge in a hurry as the new syllabus incorporates topics and lessons with which they are not quite familiar. Whether the pupils are mature enough to absorb and assimilate what they are taught or fed and whether the teachers are smart enough to elucidate advanced -content, is of little consideration. Every syllabus-revision is dreaded by teachers as they are left with little time to do home-work before venturing into the class. Both the teachers and the taught are perplexed.

Is this a laudable move? Do we have to have an overburdened curriculum? Should we fast-forward the cassette of cognitive development! Is it desirable? Is it healthy?

We need a National Debate on this vital issue. Parents need to be enlightened to "go slow" on their concern for the well-being of their sons and daughters. Above all, schooling has to be an exciting and enjoyable exploration rather than an enervating, excruciating endurance-test. Saner counsel ought to guide the policy-makers to be child-centred in their approach to curriculum construction.

"If you could not be forgotten as soon as you are dead and rotten, either write things worth reading, or do things worth the reading".

—*Benjamin Franklin.*

"When the Hon'ble member gets up to speak, he does not know what he is going to say; when he is on his feet, he does not know what he is saying; and when he sat down, he does not know what he has said.

—*Winston Churchill.*

25

On Mother

Of all the persons who shape one's life, MOTHER reigns supreme and unparalleled. Every one is kept safe and sound for ten long months in the mother's womb before delivery into the post-natal world! The world outside keeps changing while the world within a mother, in the prenatal stage, seldom changes. She silently bears the uneasiness of conception, growth and development of the fetus, the extra-weight of the baby within, along with life-supporting tissues, tubes and fluids, endures the birth-pangs of the newborn on the day of the delivery! She experiences the ecstasy of releasing the baby from captivity! Eyes of the newborn might be closed, but mouth would open automatically when the mother breast-feeds the tiny creature! Both are at peace during feeding time. She not only feeds milk, but affection, security, trust and all that one needs in life. They remain inseparable for days and days though individuation is inevitable sooner or later.

Immobility changes into crawling, later walking and running when maturation and development accelerate the process of growth from infancy into childhood, adolescence and adulthood. In no other species do we find anyone living with mother so long and so lovingly. She is tolerant of all lapses, even unpardonable lapses. Often we exploit this privilege! She is so possessive that she cannot take it too kindly when her daughter leaves the house after marriage or her son is grabbed by a strange girl whom he chose to marry. She is compelled to practise "detached attachment" as the Gita says. No wonder we call our country, `Mother-land' and the language we speak, `Mother-tongue'. Mother becomes a grandmother and great grandmother with the passing years and one always remains a child to mother regardless of age and status.

In her autobiography, ANNIE BESANT uses the choicest words to express her deep love for her mother:

"It is well to be able to look back to a mother who served as ideal of all that was noblest and dearest during childhood and girlhood, whose face made the beauty of home and whose love was both sun and shield. No other experience in life could quite make up for missing the perfect tie between mother and child- a tie that in our case never relaxed and never weakened... I have never met a woman more selflessly devoted to those she loved, more passionately contemptuous of all that was mean or base, more keenly sensitive on every question of honour more iron in will, more sweet in tenderness that the mother who made my girlhood sunny and dreamland, who guarded me, until my marriage, from every touch of pain that she could ward off or bear for me, who suffered more in every trouble that touched me in later life than I did myself."

Blessed are those blessed with such a mother!

Blessed are those blessed with such a daughter!

26

Whom Are We to Blame?

Those parents who have the onerous responsibility of sheltering adolescents at home of either sex would vouch for the enervating as well as embarrassing experiences. How could any one forget the memorable lines of Rabindranath Tagore, who, in his essay "Home Coming" describes the feelings of a fourteen-year old boy so graphically!

> "In this world of human affairs there is no worse nuisance than a boy at the age of fourteen. He is neither ornamental nor useful. It is impossible to shower affection on him as on a little boy. If he talks with a childish lisp he is called a baby, and if he answers in a grown-up way he is called impertinent. In fact any talk from him is resented. Then he is at the unattractive growing age. He grows out of his clothes with indecent haste; his voice grows hoarse and breaks and quivers; his face grows suddenly angular and unsightly. It is easy to excuse the shortcomings of early childhood, but it is hard to tolerate even unavoidable lapses in a boy of fourteen. The lad himself becomes painfully self-conscious. When he talks with elderly people he is either unduly forward or else so unduly shy that he appears ashamed of his very existence.

> Yet, it is at this very age that in his heart of hearts a young lad craves most for recognition and love and he becomes the devoted slave of any one who shows him consideration. But none dare openly love him, for, that would be regarded as undue indulgence, bad for the boy."

Though several decades have rolled by since Tagore penned the portrayal of a teen-ager, the situation remains more or less the same, if not worse!

So long one remains an infant and also a child one willingly submits to the exhortations of parents and teachers and carry out every task scrupulously and joyously too. Of course, there may be occasions in every family when an youngster is rather grouchy or negativistic. One might refuse to be tamed or trained. But, by and large, children in middle-class families hold the parents in great esteem and would never disobey or displease them. Why should there be a sudden transformation in their personality? Why should they lose their mooring and get adrift in the sea of life?

Psychologists attribute this change to several factors such as physiological maturation, heightened sensitivity, sociological changes and also the double-standards most youngsters witness at home as well as the community. They are prone to revolt and react in a manner unexpected of them by their parents. No matter how harsh and inflexible parents are, they manage to register their protest overtly or covertly.

Whom are we to blame - parents or their teen-aged progeny? There are authoritative parents who believe in their supremacy and look down upon the immaturity of youngsters. They do not realise that their authoritarianism would soon wear out. There are permissive parents who conceded to every demand be it legitimate or otherwise-

and bring up children without any restriction whatsoever. There are also parents who believe in freedom within the framework of a few 'Do's' and 'Donts' which are not pushed down the throats of youngsters but explained and persuaded to cultivate manners. Unfortunately, most parents refuse to change themselves while they are unanimous in their accusation that youngsters are aggressive, non-cooperative, and, to use the technical term, "delinquents".

Physiological maturation results in pronounced changes in their bodily contour and gives rise to a good deal of embarrassment. They tend to withdraw from strangers, remain secretive most of the time, spend a lot of time in contemplation and not at all outspoken. Parents need not entertain the notion that they have been abandoned by their own children. Not at all. They feel shy to discuss many things with their parents either out of delicacy or deference and choose to consult their own peers or someone outside the family. If only this truth is made known to parents, a lot of crushed feelings could have been averted by parents as well as their progeny.

It is true that children are submissive and compliant and look upon parents as Gods. Whatever they say would be considered sacrosanct. They rarely consider that they have their own individuality and that there is nothing wrong in harmless, outspoken discussion. Their feelings are hurt more easily during teen-age when they are ordered to do what they do not want to do. They do not wish to remain a doormat. They tend to assert and react, just to develop their will-power. When the will-power of parents become stronger the will-power of teenagers get weakened. Should we weaken their will-power? Would we not foster in them a trait, that would be more harmful to their future. Most parents, especially those practising authoritarianism, would ruthlessly put down even the slightest murmur, let alone a legitimate protest!

There has been a sea-change in the sociological set-up of late. Youngsters are exposed to a variety of stimuli that their parents had rarely encountered at their teen-age. Electronic media, Print-media and film-world have revolutionised social life beyond imagination. What was once considered impolite and improper, no more remain so. Parents cannot possibly insulate their youngsters from outside influences. Whether these influences are beneficial or harmful is an altogether different matter. Parents must be aware or made to be aware that some attitudinal changes in the teen-agers are bound to take place whether they like it or not.

There is no ready-made solution to this problem. Perhaps parents need to ensure that they remain frank and outspoken; they do not preach what they themselves cannot practise; they concede the rights of adolescents to take their own decisions with regard to their future studies, employment and also life-partner, so that they would not blame parents for their omissions and commissions!

Couple a restriction with a privilege;
Couple a liberty with a responsibility;
Couple a compliment with a criticism;
And criticism with a compliment;
Link the adolescent demands with his
learning capacity.

27

Lost Cause: Guidance Movement

An oft-quoted reference to teacher is that of a friend, philosopher and guide. When we admit our kids in a school we repose much faith in the humble teacher. We advise our children to obey their commands and commandments. Under the benevolent care of teacher children blossom and mature. They are taught a variety of subjects like Mathematics, Science, Social Studies, Mother-tongue, National language, English and also the Fine Arts. School curriculum is framed on the firm foundation of the genesis and development of human abilities. A variety of disciplines contribute to a holistic cognitive development of children. However, as children ascend to higher classes, they realise they are proficient in some and deficient in some other areas. But, everyone has to study all subjects prescribed in curricula upto SSLC. Around this stage emerges one's aptitudes. Some students may prefer Mathematics and Science, while some find History and Geography more fascinating. Some pick up languages quickly while others display their virtuosity in Fine Arts. It is a natural phenomenon.

When we plant a sapling and water it regularly, we do not decide the direction in which the branches should spread or the thickness of its trunk or even the fruits it should bear! These are predetermined. But teachers who nurture the growth and development of mental abilities of children year after year ought to be more aware of the direction in which the branches spread. To believe that one branch of studies is superior and others inferior is nothing but foolhardiness. Parents who profess and also repose so much faith in school teachers do not seem as sure about their counsel when told, "Your son/daughter would be an eminent short-story writer or a novelist or an eminent historian or sociologist. They want teachers to say the obvious - that they would blossom into top-ranking Doctors and Engineers. The lure for lucrative jobs deflects many of our bright brains to areas unrelated to their aptitudes. The sane counselling provided by teachers is sidelined by parents when it does not suit their choice of what their wards should be. This lack of faith in Teacher's counsel has rendered the Guidance Movement in our country a failure.

Just about a century ago the Guidance-Movement gathered momentum in the American soil. Industrial Revolution profoundly affected the life-style of people. There was a growing demand in the industry for the 'right' person to do the right job. Frank Parsons played the leading role in the USA. He is hailed as the 'Father of Guidance Movement'. That set in motion the support system, namely 'Mental Testing'. Not for nothing did Bennett, Seashore, and Wesman labour hard to prepare the "Differential Aptitude Test (DAT). They sought to study the aptitudes of students at school stage. E.K. Strong designed the 'Vocational Interest Blank' (SVIB) to determine pupils' interests.

The Mudaliar Commission set up by the Government of India in 1952 strongly recommended the establishment of Guidance and Counselling Services and Secondary Schools in 1954. It was reiterated by the Education Commission headed by Prof. D.S. Kothari in 1966. The Central Bureau of

Educational and Vocational guidance was established in New Delhi in 1954. It was later merged with the Department of Psychological Foundations in the NCERT, New Delhi.

For several years the Department in the NCERT offered a One-year Post-graduate Diploma course in Guidance and Counselling. The National Policy of Education (NPE-1986) underscored the importance of Guidance in Education. In spite of all these well-meaning efforts of educationists, our school authorities are yet to realise its importance and establish a Guidance wing, staffed by trained counsellors.

Meanwhile, there is a persistent flow towards certain select professions like computers and medicine. Given an opportunity all students wish to be in these professions, irrespective of the fact whether they have an aptitude for the subjects or not. Parents are the major culprits in this exodus because they systematically brain-wash their sons and daughters and thus contribute to the Brain-drain. Imagine for a moment what would have happened to R.K. Narayan had his teachers and parents coerced him to study Medicine or Engineering! He was not ashamed to be a story-writer though he took a long time to reach the peak. His brother R.K. Laxman chose to be an indifferent student so that he could make caricatures of his teachers by cartoon-drawing. His life was not an impoverished one.

Why did Salim Ali choose to wander in the country side to watch birds? Did he not become a great ornithologist? C.V. Raman resigned a well-paid Government job and chose to teach Physics. He planned his life well. Ramanujan, a failed Intermediate lad, did not remain contented with the clerical job in Madras Port Trust. His hobby of Mathematics calculation catapulted him to the heights of glory. The parents and teachers of these men did not brain-wash them to choose a particular profession. Thank God, they lived at a time when the tentacles of computer did not develop diabolically.

Instead of thrusting a profession on their children, parents should work together with the teachers and help their ward realise where his/her aptitude lies. A professional counselling centre would be an ideal platform for this. But, the Guidance Movement is doomed to fail in our country. Just count the number of schools that have employed full-time trained counsellors. Parents are also to blame for this. They would certainly rebel at the intervention of counsellors. After all, don't they presume to know better what is good for their sons and daughters?

Guidance has its positive effects, no doubt, but it may also bear an adverse effect on children. Let us enumerate the principles and malpractices of guidance:

Principle

Left to themselves and to their preceptors students are likely to decide what they should study on the basis of their realistic self-perception.

Malpractice

Never trust their capacity to choose, because, they are immature. Never allow them to examine their deficiencies. Help them overcome by hook or crook.

Principle

Encourage them to approach a teacher or counsellor who would clarify their doubts and help them understand their subjects.

Malpractice

Send them to a professional tuition-master, trained in the art of ramming. Prepare them to blindly reproduce whatever was dictated.

Principle

Monetary compensation is secondary. Self-fulfilment is primary. Choose a course of study or occupation rationally and boldly.

Malpractice

The more money you make, the higher your status in society. Forget the cliche of job-satisfaction.

Principle

Do not hesitate to branch off into Fine Arts, if you are really talented. Do not blindly join the flock of students gate-crashing into colleges of technical education.

Malpractice

You cannot make a living as a musician or a dancer or artist. You might regret. Never fall into the trap of Performing Arts.

> "There was a young lady called Bright, whose speed was faster than light. She set out one day in a relative way and returned home the previous night"
>
> —*Einstein*

28

Vocational Maturity

Compared to the birds and animals, human beings have a fairly extended period of development from Infancy to Adulthood. Each stage has some developmental tasks to be completed to ensure maturity.

We have a constitutional right and privilege to receive formal, meaningful education upto the age of fourteen years. It roughly corresponds to the end of high-school education. Some might go beyond while others would seek jobs. Those responsible for framing the curriculum for school-education should have the foresight to design a compact package almost similar to the balanced diet one needs for good health.

Languages

We live in a country where there are many regional languages. Therefore, one needs to have a mastery over language. Besides the national and the regional language we need a knowledge of English. Otherwise we would remain like a frog in the well.

Communicative ability-written and spoken-throws open a variety of jobs for any person, be it journalism, Law, Teaching or as a Salesman, a Doctor or an Engineer. One may have to go to rural areas and address the villagers in their own mother-tongue regarding up infectious disease, Environmental cleanliness and so on.

Those who could communicate well have an edge over those who are poor communicators. If one's job takes him beyond his State he should be proficient in the language that binds people together. We should encourage children to be fluent in more than one language.

Early Lessons

Psychologists are of the opinion that a child has the capability of learning more than one language. We should exploit this. The ability to think, reason and judge correctly is a God-given gift. But, it will not develop unless one deliberately cultivates and exercises it. Needless to add how indispensable these abilities are for effective living!

Curriculum-framers have included Science and Mathematics in School education precisely for this purpose. One wonders at the genius of Ramanujan, the mathematical prodigy. One is thrilled by the inventions and discoveries of scientists like J.C. Bose, C.V. Raman, Homi Bhaba, Newton, Einstein, Graham Bell and so on. Each one demonstrated the value of scientific temper. Each one had abundant curiosity.

Opportunities

A study of Science opens up many avenues of vocation. One could be a physician, a physicist, an entomologist, an architect, a computer specialist, or a science teacher! Let us not commit the folly of forming a hierarchy and instal one above the others. Imagine how miserable life would have become if every other person were to be a Physician or a Computer specialist. We would have a surplus and that surplus would impoverish society. We do not consider 'rice' superior to 'sooji' or bringal better than beans. Don't we need all these to make life worth living! Let us, therefore, foster the scientific temper among students so that they could choose an area for specialisation after general education.

We need a sound body as well. Hitherto, I mentioned areas that predominantly belong to the cognitive domain. We have muscles and sense organs. Don't we cheer the athletes in a sportsmeet? Don't we feel proud that our Leander Paes brought a bronze-medal from the Olympic games? Don't we feel elated when Geet Sethi won the billiards championship? Curriculum framers realised the value of sports and games in the development of personality. Instead of becoming slaves of the Cable TV we should go out and play vigorous games. It would be quite refreshing.

Schooling

As parents we should always urge youngsters to enjoy schooling, like every subject and postpone vocational selection till maturation. Vocational maturity is related to emotional and intellectual maturity. One should not decide hastily and regret late. After all every teacher in school is a specialist in his own discipline. Is it not unfair to look upon -A- as superior and look down upon -B- as inferior, just because A and B teach different subjects? If, as parents, we realise this truth, we would be laying the foundation for a meaningful life for our children.

> "A man doesn't know what true happiness is until he gets married and then it is too late."
>
> —*Bernard Shaw.*

29

Something to Look For...

Findings of Psychology tell us that human Intelligence originates as a general mental ability that is fed by nutrients such as language, computation, cause-and-effect relationship, memorisation and appreciation till about the fourteenth year. Hence, a common curriculum is provided for all children upto SSLC so that the multi-dimensional aspect of intelligence is taken cognizance of.

However, as one ascends the ladder of schooling, somewhere around the age of 10 or 11, one notices an inclination to study, enjoy and profit from one or two disciplines among his school subjects. It cannot be taken as a crystallized, mature choice based on one's awareness of nature. At best, it can be construed as an act of exploration of one's real interests and aptitudes. These would still be in their incipient stages and perhaps the necessity to study a number of independent disciplines might come in the way of focussing upon a few.

By the time a student reaches the school-final stage, he would, more or less, have made up his mind whether he should opt for humanities or sciences. Here again, it remains broad-based for a couple of years, lending scope for further limitation into fields such as English, Economics, History, Sociology or Commerce under Humanities; Physics,

Mathematics, Chemistry and Biology, under Sciences. Yet, he has 'per force' to study a constellation of interrelated disciplines notwithstanding his exclusive interest and aptitude in one or two subjects.

At this point he realises he is in a forked-road situation with choices open for professional courses such as Engineering, Medicine, Agriculture and Commerce and for general education courses like Arts and Sciences.

In our society there is a tacit notion that Medicine and Engineering constitute the apex of professions and therefore the best of brains have to gravitate toward that direction. It is true that doctors and engineers play a significant role in society while it is not true that others play an insignificant role!

Let us see the aspirations of the parents for a moment. Parents of children with above average intelligence visualise a bright future for their wards either in Medicine or Engineering. Hence, a good deal of brainwashing is systematically perpetrated on young minds that they should strive hard to realise the parental ambitions. Parents worry over the grades and marks much more than the students themselves because any regression in grades is likely to influence adversely their possible entry into these prestigious professions. In this rat-race everyone ignores the natural and spontaneous liking of the youngsters! They are constantly prodded to mirror the aims and aspirations of parents rather than pursuing a course of studies they really desire!

What is the basis of the choice of such professional courses? Very few would admit frankly that it assures them a lucrative career, heightened status and possibly a considerable demand in the matrimonial market too! If the aim is to be imbued with a zeal of Sir M. Viswes-waraiah or Dr. Rangachari in doing Yeomen services to society, zealous youngsters would readily fall in line. But, a really brilliant student may have to crush his desire to study pure sciences like Theoretical Physics or Pure Mathematics for the simple reason he is not assured of a secure future! What if? An Einstein or a Raman or a Tolstoy never had such designs for a rosy future. Did they not plunge themselves into a world of their own and exercise their free-will unfettered by parental designs?

Is it true that everyone who joins an Engineering College or a Medical College turns out to be a successful engineer or doctor? The mushrooming of these professional colleges and the extortion of phenomenal capitation fees have polluted the academic climate in our country to such an extent that many bright students regret the choice of their studies midway through the course. Quite a number of them feel that they ought to have exercised their options and opted out of such professional courses. The National Laboratories in our country need fertile brains to conduct researchers of far-reaching significance.

Sometime ago, we invited a young, bright probationary officer of a Nationlised Bank to address the students on the employment opportunities in Banking Services. Basically a man of English Literature, he was lured by the emoluments and promotional prospects in Banking and sat for the Competitive Banking Examination. Selected and trained for more than three or four years, he could give a graphic picture of the career opportunities in Banks. At the end of the talk he confessed in confidence that he did not really enjoy his work. He felt that his talents and capacities were not put to proper use and that he had to do such insipid clerical work that would not warrant high academic qualifications! He said he had to stick on purely for the attractive pay and fringe benefits offered.

Is not his placement in a Bank a terrible loss to the academic world? He might have blossomed as an eminent Professor and a Creative writer too! When all his energies are sucked and sapped in totalling and tallying and signing, he returns home thoroughly exhausted and disgusted. He becomes a "Cog in the wheel" as Bertrand Russell would put it. Has he something to look for in life?

"All men are born free and equal. But some get married".

—Bernard Shaw.

"Constitutional stability is the bed rock which remains although a wave of minister may come and go"

—N.A. Palkhivala.

30

The Road Not Taken...

I am not a teacher of English. But, I had an opportunity to observe an English Poetry lesson handled by a senior teacher in a Higher Secondary Class. It was a poem by Robert Frost, titled The Road Not Taken. It runs thus:

"Two roads diverged in a yellow wood
And sorry I would not travel both.
And be one traveller, long I stood
And looked down one as far as I could
To where it bent in the undergrowth.

I took the one less travelled by
And that has made all the difference"

The teacher (a middle aged lady) simply hypnotised the class by her diction, intonation and above all, her devotion to the profession of teaching. There was lively interaction with students all through. She was able to convey the message, namely the dilemma faced by everyone in choosing the path of life in a forked road situation. Most people choose the safe path to plenty, prosperity and peace. Yet, one cannot help casting a lingering look upon the deserted road and even ruminate whether one should have taken the alternate route. Life is short. Like a river it always flows in one direction. It never flows backwards. One has to weigh the pros and cons before choosing one's vocation in life.

I rated her teaching as something remarkable, worthy of emulation. Her facile flow of language coupled with explicit excitement, meaningful gestures impressed me a great deal. I complimented her profusely. I felt that her students were extremely fortunate to be blessed with such an excellent teacher. Every student was attenative. Being a student of Psychology, I felt I should elicit the reactions of students - their aspirations and ambitions in life.

I sought the permission of the teacher and took the platform. I asked the students how they enjoyed the lesson. They were unanimous in their appreciation and adoration of their teacher. They were really thrilled! I was not surprised at the crescendo of encomiums showered upon the teacher. I asked them to take a sheet of paper and fill in according to my oral instructions. I asked them to give the name, age, father's profession, address and finally the profession they look forward to in life! Actually I was interested only in the last column!

Believe it or not, an overwhelming majority of students opted for computer engineering so as to become soft-ware specialists! The rest desired to be medical doctors. Not even a single student in the class expressed the desire to be a teacher like their teacher! Has the teacher taken the "road less travelled"?

The teacher wasn't upset, but kept smiling upon the stark reality of life. I learnt later that she was a B.SC., B.T., a teacher of Science, who volunteered to teach English because she loved it! It was heartwarming to me to be blessed with an opportunity to meet such a committed, conscientious teacher!

While leaving the school I ruminated over the kind of brainwashing that most youngsters are subjected to at home as well as the peer-group pressure, to opt for a safer path in life that guarantees prosperity. Yes! Bill Gates in rated superior to Robert Frost!

I couldn't help recalling the memorable words of Richard Bach - the gypsy pilot who shot into limelight by his epoch-making book, "Jonathan Livingston Seagull." To quote him:

> "Every individual should live a life on the basis of his own convictions make his own rules when he believes them to be right and obtain the highest pleasure of executing his life-style not according to the laws imposed by society but by the norms created by his own individuality."

"The wisdom of the wise is an uncommon degree of common sense."

—*Dean Inge.*

"Ignorance is preferable to error, and he is less remote from truth who believes nothing, than he who believes what is wrong".

—*Thomas Jefferson.*

31

The Etiology of Juvenile Delinquency

Looking retrospectively, every grown-up individual is liking to remember, perhaps with a feeling of nostalgia the prolonged period of dependency during his infant and childhood years, the gradual emancipation during adolescence, culminating in the integrative adulthood. The transition is not a smooth-sailing process, because one will have to weather many a storm all along the developmental pathway. HAVIGHURST enumerates a number of DEVELOPMENTAL TASKS characteristic of each sequential stage, the successful accomplishment of which enables one to ascend and reach higher levels of maturity. Right from birth, an individual is influenced by several agencies such as home, play-groups, school and community, each playing a distinct role in transforming the impulsive nature of the newborn into an enlightened individuality. In the absence of this transformation, perhaps mankind would have regressed to the level of beasts!

It would be appropriate here to recount in brief the views of SIGMUND FREUD, an eminent Psychoanalyst. Freud distinguished three aspects of human personality, namely, ID, EGO and SUPEREGO. ID refers to the primitive urges and passionate impulses characteristic of the infant stage.

An infant seldom distinguishes 'good' from 'bad' and is always at the mercy of his momentary impulses. Contacts with the world of objects and persons restrain him from uninhibited behaviour. He learns to come to terms with reality and also control his impulsive behaviour. This represents the origin of EGO. To assist the development of EGO, parents and teachers prescribe certain codes of conduct. A child can violate these codes only at the risk of losing the love and support of parents. Thus, the individual learns to incorporate within his SELF a series of Do's and DONTS. This is roughly equivalent to the formation of CONSCIENCE, which in Freudian terminology is called the SUPEREGO. While the ID always operates on "Pleasure Principle" the EGO Controls and regulates behaviour on "Reality Principle". The superego checks the impulses of the ID, thereby acting as the individual's conscience-keeper. What would happen to the individual when the ID becomes more powerful than the forces of EGO and SUPEREGO? That, perhaps, explains the genesis of delinquency.

Delinquency is an expression of aggression in socially disapproved ways. It is a reactive, impulsive endeavour to find direct or substitute satisfaction for natural urge. It may be construed as a kind of rebellion of the youth against the established social order. It is most pronounced during the period of adolescence when the impetuous youth tend to view the rules and regulations as an encroachment upon individual freedom and liberty. Society can function smoothly only when all the members conform to the codes of conduct, written as well as unwritten. A host of terminologies like teen-age culture, new-wave, generation gap and so on have widened the gulf between adults and adolescents and alienated the youth from the mainstream of society. To be able to understand the dynamics of delinquent behaviour, one has to probe into the basic psychological needs of the individual and find out whether these needs are adequately met or not during the formative years.

One of the basic psychological needs that contributes to the well-being of the individual is security. It is fostered by parents in the home-atmosphere by proper upbringing. A child, who is deprived of love and affection at home, would feel highly insecure and he is likely to carry over this feeling to the world outside. Case-studies of delinquents reveal that, by and large, they emerge from broken homes and unhappy families. What is significant in a broken home for the genesis of delinquency is not simply the fact of the separation, desertion, divorce or remarriage of parents, but conditions of neglect, poverty and tension accompanying such situations. Deprived of love and acceptance they tend to be suspicious of not only people at home but of everyone outside. They do not develop a sense of belongingness. They feel alienated not only from home but also from society.

Another important need that promotes healthy development is Freedom. Some may be totally deprived of freedom while others may be left free to act as they wish in an unbriddled fashion. ALFRED ADLER, the famous Psychoanalyst says that parents can spoil a child either by granting unlimited freedom or withholding it altogether. In the former case, children, having grown accustomed to act as they like at home, without any kind of control whatsoever, would expect similar patronising conditions outside home as well. Lacking in self-restraint, such children are likely to become petulant and rapacious when events turn contrary to their whims and fancy. In the other extreme, children, having been subjected to rigid discipline and control and deprived of even basic freedom tend to be inhibited not only at home but also outside. They would remain suspicious, withdrawn and uncommunicative. According to Adler, these STYLES OF LIFE would remain permanent characteristics of individuals and act as predisposing factors for delinquent behaviour.

Need for recognition and status is another important factor in the building of self-esteem. Every child, irrespective of his accomplishment, craves for recognition. In various ways children strive to build their self-image and status. In some families, children are either ignored or always unfavourably compared with the smarter ones from the neighbourhood. Consequently, a negative-self-image is developed, which ultimately results in a feeling of despair and worthlessness. Having failed to attain status and recognition of home, such individuals might seek recourse to deviant means of satisfying this urge. They tend to indulge in acts of violence and excitement, presumably to arrest the attention of onlookers!

One of the manifestations of delinquent behaviour is truancy. A truant is one who runs away from school and sometimes from home also. It is a delinquent behaviour in so far as it represents a disregard of the main request which society makes of a child, namely school attendance. Children might resort to truancy in order to be able to enjoy their daydreams which are interrupted at home and school. It is frequently the potential delinquent's first break with established family discipline and authority. Successful acts of initial truancy may induce other violations of established rules. Provocative movies and pornographic novels might incite the evil propensities of the youth to indulge in something sensational and to become a villain. By being a truant an individual registers his resentment toward parents and teachers. He craves for emancipation from family bonds and rigid school schedule.

Delinquent styles change with the same rapidity as other fashions. In recent times drug-addiction has increased among the youth. Heroin, Marijuana, amphetamines, barbiturates and hallucinogenic drugs are used by delinquents for intoxicating effects. Apart from the harmful effects of addiction to the individual and his consequent social disorganization, the illegality that attaches to drug use creates a small but complete subculture of user and pusher, of time spent in raising (often stealing) the necessary money, and in finding the supply.

Delinquency is essentially a social malady. It is caused mainly by social conditions which thwart the satisfaction of the basic needs of the individual. Actually, no delinquent has a gene - or a set of genes - that produce in him a tendency to indulge in antisocial behaviour. People are less interested in attacking the problem of delinquency than in attacking the delinquent himself. Prescriptions for dealing with delinquency often seem to be designed more for revenge than for prevention or reform. The average citizen, preoccupied with his own problems of daily life, seldom reacts to episodes of delinquency with any degree of objectivity and understanding. An informed and objective citizenry is a prerequisite to effective social planning.

The shocking truth is that very often, adults are instrumental to the spread of delinquency among the youth. The pornographic outlets, the crime -comic publishing houses and the call-girl rackets are not controlled by teen-age monsters. These are run by adults who publicise the delinquent as a heartless, sex-crazy, rapacious, conscienceless and monstrous character with a lurid picture on the cover to sell paperbacks. Thus portrayed, the delinquent has great sales-value as a means by which the reader can find a vicarious outlet for aggressive impulses and sexual desires. Frequently it is an inaccurate and exaggerated fabrication. The distorted picture begins to actualize itself when youngsters begin to act out what they have seen.

Most citizens live in the hope and expectation that eventually some outside authority, institution or agency will come to the rescue and solve-with something of magic if not money - the problem of juvenile delinquency. They generally omit or exclude the most important player - the youth himself. In a sense, only delinquents can solve the delinquency problem. But, they are seldom consulted in the study, planning and implementation of programmes for delinquency prevention!

Leon Eisenberg in his working paper for the W.H.O. Expert Committee in Geneva on the Health Problems of Adolescence remarked that,

> "No society can hope to survive, let alone improve itself, that does not succeed in harnessing the constructive, searching supra-personal and supra-national drives of the adolescent. The capacity for engagement in meaningful social activity is clearly present in young people in every country in the world. The challenge to the behavioural scientist is to help his own country develop the forms and means to enable the adolescent to take a leading role in the struggle for the attainment of a world in which peace, freedom and economic opportunity are available to all."

32

Personality on Sale!

A recent spate of self-styled "Behaviour Therapists" claim they can transform the `personality' of any person by an exquisitely designed `Personality-Development' programme. Their claim is that they have conducted these courses as `Yagnas' in remote Gulf-countries and the innumerable testimonies of unseen clients! Many, seeking instant success indiscreetly fall victim to such alluring advertisements and lose their hard-earned money. It is ironical that these `pseudo-psychologists' outnumber genuine ones. One who has studied the discipline of Psychology would not venture to make extravagant claims of being able to turn baser metals into gold like an alchemist!

Referring a psychology book would be mind-boggling at best. Volumes on the agreements and disagreements, the latter being more than the former, are numerous. There are "Type-approaches" and "Trait approaches". Both approaches may be at loggerheads at times. Perhaps it is easier to understand the meaning of a statement such as, "X is a good person" than "X has a good personality". One who is honest, hard-working, helpful, kind, trustworthy, punctual and pleasant is undoubtedly a good person. Few would dispute this statement. But, when you use the word `personality' as an abstraction, you are in for trouble. To describe someone as "wonderful, charismatic, magnetic, vivacious" would be meaningless because these prefixes lack precision and definiteness. Perhaps it would be prudent to abandon the use of the term `Personality' and instead use the term `Person'.

Carl Rogers' book titled "On Becoming a Person" is devoted to the development of a person-as self-confident, secure, self-reliant person, capable of pulling his/her own weight, deciding individually and also realistically on various issues, being aware of one's shortcomings as well as assets, assertive but not aggressive.

Rogers did not conduct "one-week personality development" programmes in America. According to him development is longitudinal like a bud that becomes a flower and eventually a fruit. Unlike a plant, human beings have to strive hard to forge human behaviour. It is no cake-walk!

Memory, creativity, confidence, leadership and several behavioural characteristics are the products of years of sustained effort, practice and commitment. These are not available for 'over-the-counter' sales. Newton's Law of Motion or the painting skills of Leonardo da Vinci cannot be acquired by a pill or a short-term brainstorming session. But, if one were to be serious, it would not be difficult to be a good person. A person's height, complexion, texture of hair, colour of eyes are genetically, transmitted traits. Honesty and cheerfulness are not. These are acquired in a social environment. A psychologist whose wares are "on sale" is dubious. Psychologists are not salesmen. They do not make extravagant claims. Nor do they cash in with projects of 'Personality Development'!

33

Personality Development

Since the dawn of civilization man has been curious to know himself and his hidden nature. Several parties began the exploration of the dark continent of the elusive PSYCHE-PERSONALITY - either in small groups or solitarily and came back with their own perceptions and interpretations. Everyone is fascinated by the term 'Personality' as it is likely to determine one's success in life. Exploiting the human weakness, quite a number of charlatans have been advertising Personality-Development programmes that would enhance one's self-confidence, motivation, memory power, creativity, leadership qualities and a host of traits. There are plenty of self-improvement books, the most popular ones being Dale Carnegie's "How to Win Friends" and "How to Stop Worrying and Start Living". It is good to remember the saying, "Rome is not built in a day." Nor is Personality developed through a crash course!

Personality is not an inborn endowment but an acquired disposition arising out of constant interacting with people around. Since birth every human being is interacting with a variety of people and every experience leaves an imprint on one's personality. Mother, Father, brothers, sisters, friends—all influence the development of a child. Whereas an animal develops quite fast and functions autonomously within a few years, human beings have a prolonged period of development — Infancy, childhood, adolescence and adulthood. This extended span is necessary for the acquisition of skills, knowledge and attitude that comprise one's personality. As an infant, one is egocentric (Self-centred) and while one grows one gets socialised by extending his feeling of "I" into "We". One realises that one cannot lead a balanced, harmonious life without giving up a part of one's self for the society that protects him.

Psychoanalysis: Sigmund Freud

Sigmund Freud laid the foundation-stone for the analysis and description of the Psychodynamics of Personality. He introduced three important terms, namely ID, EGo and SUPEREGO. ID represents the untamed, uncivilised, blind instinctual impulses, always seeking immediate gratification, regardless of social approval or disapproval. During infancy, parents are usually permissive and tolerant and hence ID enjoys freedom of expression. ID is governed by "Pleasure Principle". As one moves from Infancy to childhood a perceptible change in behaviour emerges. World of Reality subdues the ID and thus the EGo or the SELF emerges. A lid over ID is essential for Personality-development. The Ego is governed by "Reality Principle".

Living in a society necessitates the observance of social codes and cultural values. Parents tend to instil in children codes of conduct perhaps gently to start with. As years pass by, grown-ups realise that violation of the family-code would be met with punishment. Children tend to feel guilty whenever they violate the family-code. Freud termed this moral frame of reference the SUPEREGO. It helps an individual to discriminate right from wrong acts. When a child receives punishment for his lapses he develops what is called CONSCIENCE. Whenever he receives praise for approved behaviour, EGO-IDEAL is formed. This incorporation or internalization of the social expectation within one's self is termed INTROJECTION by Freud. A weakened ego and superego would strengthen the ID that would spell catastrophe in society. A good home, a disciplined school and an integrated community-life would foster healthy attitudes and contribute toward wholesome personality development.

Alfred Adler

Alfred Adler, a disciple of Freud, gave importance to the SELF-ASSERTIVE impulse. Every individual strives for power and mastery. The child resists domination and tries to dominate over others. At the same time the child is also conscious of its inferiority. The inferiority arises out of immaturity in contrast to the maturity and competency of adults around. But, the child is not prepared to accept this. On the other hand, he tries to put on a SUPERIOR false-front to conceal his inner feelings of INFERIORITY. Naturally, this causes strain to the individual and to some extent might result in Personality-maladjustment.

Adler is well-known for introducing the phrase STYLE OF LIFE. It refers to a pattern of living formed during early childhood, that prepares the ground for well-adjusted or maladjusted personality. The home-environment is the potent factor in shaping one's style of life. Parents could shower affection upon their child to such an extent that he becomes a SPOILED CHILD. Too much PAMPERING is not good. Such a child finds it difficult to adjust to the demands of real life. A child whose every wish has been gratified, who has received all the attention exclusively, finds the outside world quite different. That means he is not sufficiently prepared to face life.

Supposing a child has been punished frequently. He is always on the defensive and feels insecure. Such a child would look upon the world outside with a feeling of hostility and distrust. He cannot develop a sense of belongingness. Both the types of life are ill-suited to the world of reality. Such a condition arises purely out of poor upbringing. Therefore, parents should neither be too permissive nor to restrictive in their dealings with children.

Carl Jung

Another disciple of Freud, Carl Jung, identified two dimensions of Personality; namely Extraversion and Introversion. An extrovert is one whose interests and energies are primarily channelled toward outside world of objects and persons, who makes friendship easily, displays sociability as well as leadership qualities and is a man of action. On the other hand, an introvert is mostly preoccupied with his own inner world of thinking and imagination, avoiding company of others and publicity and also displaying a certain amount of shyness and reservation. While these represent two extremes, some, if not most people, fall mid-way between the two and they are called Ambiverts. However, the choice of one's vocation is to a considerable extent related to the personality-factor. An introvert is likely to be a poor salesman or a business-executive. But, he could be a wonderful teacher, poet and philosopher.

Humanistic School of Thought

Carl Rogers and Abraham Maslow firmly believe in the basic, positive side of human behaviour. Under favourable conditions personality unfolds spontaneously and magnificently. Unwholesome influences tend to deflect the course of personality development. Both the above psychologists have contributed a great deal in the area of COUNSELLING and PSYCHOTHERAPY. Rogers is well-known for his NON-DIRECTIVE COUNSELLING while MASLOW is known for his theory of SELF-ACTUALIZATION. Both of them reflect the views of SWAMI

VIVEKANANDA, who looked upon Education as "the manifestation of perfection already in man".

Personality Traits

Personality is essentially a social concept. For instance, when we say Mr. X is withdrawn, ascendant, co-operative, friendly, assertive, it is always with reference to a social medium. Psychologists use the term Traits to the qualities listed above. One may possess a number of traits. These traits have some unity-an integration. For instance, a person is not only cheerful but also self-reliant. A healthy personality in an Integrated personality. Picture to yourself individuals with the following traits.

A = Energetic, assured, talkative, Cold, ironical, inquisitive, persuasive.

B = Energetic, assured, talkative, Warm, ironical, inquisitive, persuasive.

Inspite of a difference in only one trait, the total personality changes a lot!

To quote Aldous Huxley:

> "Perhaps the most valuable result of all education is the ability to make yourself do the thing you have to do, when it ought to be done, whether you like it or not. However early a man's training begins, it is probably the last lesson that he learns thoroughly."

34

Attachment-Detachment

Life originates in attachment, grows in it, survives in it and when gets detached from its primary source of sustenance still continues to get attached despite physical detachment from the donor! How long, how far, how much - are the basic issues of life and living.

After ten long months of maternal odyssey, the five-pound bundle of tissues and tubes peeps out of the mother's womb. With the cutting of the umbilical cord, the visitor to the postnatal world of 'booming, buzzing confusion' is simply dazzled'. Soon, the little creature makes the first birth-cry. Why should it cry? Why should the mother also cry? Soon 'cries' turned out to be 'laughs' from everyone, except for the newborn, that continues to cry, cry and cry.

Otto Rȧnk is gifted with fertile imagination. He postulates two kinds of Fear-Life-Fear and Death-Fear. Having been accustomed to a kind of care-free life due to the symbiotic bond with the mother during the prenatal stage, the progeny is reluctant to relinquish the union and face separation. Mother also is equally unwilling to part with the baby though she was able to bear the burden, sickness feelings etc, etc, for what seemed to her, eternity. The newborn is scared of the Life outside the chamber it occupied. Does it experience a longing to get back to the place of origin? Is it possible?

What would happen if one were to attempt this crazy move? The baby would die of asphyxiation. Hence, there is a fear of Death. Inability to reconcile the 'Life-fear' and 'Death-fear' is the dilemma of life.

Let us accompany the baby to the eighteenth milestone of life. All these years, the newborn has traversed through, Infancy, childhood and Adolescence. All his/her needs were fulfilled by parents at home.

A day comes when the young girl may have to leave home, to stay in a far off place-hostel attached to a college. It would be a painful separation. The girl finds the new environment unfamiliar, unfriendly and unsuitable. She longs to be back home. Parents too miss her much. Both, however, have to overcome this temptation. If the girl decides to yield to her urge to get back home, she misses the opportunity to detach herself from parental fold and enjoy her independence. She learns to be self-reliant and autonomous. Parents need to encourage her to get detached. Does she not bid farewell to her parents when she gets married and accompanies her husband?

Detachment invariably follows attachment. Ripe mangoes fall, trees shed off leaves during autumn. New leaves emerge during spring. Cow gives birth to calf. Calf cannot remain with her mother long. There is no place for sentimentalism. Each one must learn to be independent. It doesn't mean forsaking parents. For the sake of their children and their future, parents ought to teach them to practise Detached Attachment.

35

Behaviour in the Classroom and Beyond

Just observe the behaviour of tinytots as well as grown-ups half-an-hour before the commencement of the morning session. Absolutely unpretentious, totally relaxed, they seem to be full of life, looking forward to an exciting day at school. They run around, play hide and seek, quarrel a little and get united soon. Home cannot provide such a joyous atmosphere. No child can afford to miss this heavenly abode of a good school!

A long bell is the signal for everyone to suspend their playful pranks, be good and smart, march in a line from their respective classes to what is called "Morning Assembly". They are "conditioned" to obey commands such as "Attention", "Stand-at-ease " and so on, whether they like it on not. Prayer begins with a group of girls standing before the microphone. The whole congregation would join the lead-performers in a crescendo. Synchronization is impossible when about a thousand voices render the same lines in varied scales. A few announcements by the Head or Newspaper headlines from a bold student followed by the singing of the National Anthem closes the morning Assembly. They disperse and march into their classes in a line.

Until the teacher steps into the class students continue to enjoy some limited freedom to mix and mingle. The entry of the teacher transforms the atmosphere instantly, incredibly. Not a whisper perhaps. Some might exchange glances about the dress of the teacher. If a teacher is really interested in behaviour-modification of students he/she need not encourage or support such a military-like discipline or orderliness. It is a kind of facade that conceals their true nature. It is likely to vanish sooner when the teacher leaves the class. Not that the teacher should permit pandemonium or disorder. He/she should be a little permissive or tolerant without being taken for a ride! If at such an young age students cannot enjoy freedom when at all would they have this privilege! Allow a child to be a child, and do not make them miniature adults!

Supposing a science teacher introduces the lesson on "Plants" in a primary class, "You see, there are countless plants and trees, much more than human beings on this good earth. On your way to school you might have observed several of them. Little ones are called "Plants". Huge ones are called "Trees". All plants do not become trees. Little ones are proud of their multicoloured flowers and different kind of leaves. There is no jealousy among them. They remain friendly. They seem to enjoy life and bright sunshine. You and I may seek a shade to rest and relax, but plants welcome sunrays joyously. They do not get scorched or famished. They drink water from the ground through their roots. Plants are deeprooted. You cannot uproot them so easily. Let us discuss today the affinity between plants and sunlight. On a cloudy day you and I may heave a sigh of relief because we escape the heat, but plants observe a kind of mourning with drooping leaves and motionless nature! They seem to be depressed because the sun is shielded by clouds! Listen to Joyce Kilmore:

I think I shall never see a poem as lovely as a tree
A tree whose hungry mouth is prest against the earth's sweet flowing breast
A tree that looks at God all day
And lifts her leafy arms to pray.
Poems are made by fools like me
But only God can make a tree.

This is just an illustration to commence a lesson to a third grade class to introduce the concept of "Photosynthesis". In spiral curriculum, according to Bruner, concepts are presented to students at assimilable levels of abstraction. In higher classes they get enriched and expanded.

Children enjoy interactive sessions than monotonous monologues. Informal teaching results in better learning than rigid, authoritative instruction. This holds good at all levels. Behaviour-modification cannot take place by rewarding passivity and docility and punishing genuine curiosity and activity. Lessons must be taught in such a way that, forty-five minutes pass like forty-five seconds.

Invariably teacher must suggest a follow-up activity to be done at home. It need not necessarily be a stereotyped written one. Variety would generate interest. Teacher should not expect every student to be bold, cheerful, smart and industrious. A class consists of heterogeneous mix of temperaments. Skilfully handled, a teacher can succeed to a great extent in modifying the behaviour of the hesitant, reticent students into a lively nature. There is always a spill-over from the outside world beyond classroom. If only the barbed wires are removed and a free zone is created without check-posts most of the minor behavioural problems would disappear.

36

Baby Also Feels...

I am only three. But, my mummy says I'm grown-up and I'm no more a baby! I am told, I have no business to stay at home beyond 8 o'clock. Of course, I would be back for lunch. I am dressed up in a hurry. My tiny feet get pushed into socks and shoes. I cannot take my own time to eat breakfast leisurely. I am hustled and huddled into a school-van that honks precisely at eight every morning. I wait impatiently at the gate for the yellow-painted van. It is already filled with babies of my age who look through the glass window. I join them. Some are sobbing, some remain abnormally quiet and some enact fighting scenes of comics they saw in TV. I am in a dilemma. What should I do?

My parents have taken infinite pains to admit me into a place called 'school'. I don't know what it means! There are many rooms. I find tiny ones like me and also big brothers and sisters. There is a small open space to assemble in the morning, and play in the evening. I am supposed to remain only in one particular classroom. I find a few toys, and quite a few things that I cannot name. A strange lady greets us. I am told she is our teacher. She is nicely dressed. But, every now and then, she raises her voice and says, "keep quiet!" I find it difficult to keep quiet. It is not in my nature. I always make noise at home. I look at others in my class. We look at each other. We suffer in silence!

Our teacher sings what she calls "Nursery rhymes". I do not know what it means. We are asked to sing in chorus. We do so in full-throated voice. Our teacher tells stories also. But, they are boring. We are forced to listen. Some yawn, and some pretend to listen. We find it difficult to stay motionless for long hours. But, we are forced to remain so. We feel uncomfortable. We are told we will become great by reading books. It sounds hollow. We hear the long bell - the bell we eagerly await! We rush out to occupy a window seat in the van. My mother swells with pride upon seeing me in school uniform, bag and water bottle! She asks me about my school. I say, `It is fine!' I don't mean what I say! Who cares for my feelings?

"The man who goes alone can start today, but he who travels with another must wait until the other is ready"

— *Henry David Thoreau.*

37

Behaviour-Modification I

I am an ordinary mother, a housewife, a pragmatist — all rolled into one. I hold myself, to some extent, responsible for my children's behaviour. My four children - two of each sex-displayed divergent behaviours. That made comparison difficult. I cannot say I was all that successful in modifying their behaviour. I used to be harsh on them sometimes. They would just brush me aside. To a considerable extent, schooling modified their behaviour a great deal. Their dress, manners, speech, study-habits and hobbies - all underwent a slow, gradual change. Perhaps peer-group interaction modified their behaviour. What a mother struggled to achieve and gave up, schooling did admirably!.

Teachers, particularly in lower classes, influence children a great deal. I remember my daughters recounting how a particular teacher- a nun- had a subtle but kind and firm control over mischievous kids. Children did not panic, but took liberties with that teacher. Not that she permitted pandemonium in her class. She wasn't authoritarian, anyway. She was a benevolent authority, not a tyrannical teacher. She would make kids reflect and correct themselves. Never did she humiliate them. She was only a second standard teacher. I do not think she would have read books on "Behaviour Modification". She did it in her own intuitive way!

Once I went to school to know from her the secret of her success. She was warm and friendly. She was overjoyed to meet me. Perhaps very few parents cared to meet her and thank her. I never subjected her to a question-answer session. I just sought her permission to watch her class from the corridor. She readily consented.

Upon her very presence all children's faces brightened up. She held a book, Radiant Reader. What an appropriate title for that age-group! The teacher herself was radiant. An incandescent smile was ever-present upon her face. Children in her class had never seen her furious on any occasion. She became a role-model for children. She wouldn't be upset if some chuckle in her class. She taught them the magic of influencing others. Did she not have any occasion to be angry or frustrated? When most teachers have plenty of grievances of all kinds, how could this teacher be an exception?

I complimented her at the end of the class for her exemplary teaching. I couldn't talk to her exclusively, because all kids swarmed her even after the bell. They followed her like the rats in the "Pied Piper of Hamelin"! She was struggling to disentangle herself from the kids. What a mother could not do, some teachers do effortlessly!

My daughters are no more kids. They have kids of their own! They still cherish nostalgic memories of their primary school days with that teacher. More than two decades have rolled by. Are my daughters paying their gratitude to their teacher? Yes! Both my daughters teach - one at the post-graduate level, another at the primary level. My daughter-in-law too teaches in a college. They have grown-up students in their classes. Do they emulate their teacher? I guess, they do. Some teaches surpass mothers in child upbringing. While most mothers find it impossible to bring up two or three at home, how could a teacher like this nun influence so many in a class simultaneously? I wonder how that teacher would react if she were to meet my daughters now - after a gap of twenty-five years!

> "Robert Boyle once said that it is highly dishonourable for a Reasonable Soul to live in so divinely built a mansion as the Body she resides in, altogether unacquainted with the exquisite structure of it."
>
> "Sin is not hurtful because it is forbidden, but it is forbidden because it is hurtful. Nor is a duty beneficial because it is commanded, but it is commanded because it is beneficial."
>
> — *Benjamin Franklin*

38

Behaviour-Modification II: Myths and Realities!

The subject of Psychology has caught the attention of almost every literate person. It has charisma! As a Behavioural Science it is quite a serious, systematic discipline. One who has undergone a regular, rigorous course in Psychology in an established university seldom boasts of his/her capacity to achieve miracles in the transformation of an individual's personality. For example, a layman would not venture to speak with authority on sedimentary rocks or alluvial soil unless he had studied Geology. Nor would one comment upon Atomic Science or Electromagnetism unless he had undergone a foundation course in Physics. To speak on Shakespeare's plays or the contrasting poetic styles of T.S. Eliot and Wordsworth one ought to have done a serious study of English Literature.

Paradoxically, we have grown accustomed to tolerate, if not promote, hundreds and thousands of charlatans or quacks, masquerading as experts in "Behaviour-modification"! Would a genuine psychologist ever proclaim to improve your personality or Creativity or Memory or self-confidence in about a few hours of pep-talks or funny exercises! But, a pseudo-psychologist would claim mystic powers to achieve this miracle for a price. As there is no shortage of gullible persons in the world one can always lure them through spurious advertisements. Many people do not mind spending their valuable time and money in such worthless pursuits, only to realise late, that they were taken for a ride! Law does not seem to prohibit the proliferation of such cheats who are doing a roaring business in "Personality-change".

We must clear ourselves of some of the myths and misconceptions in current usage. Supposing a person is by nature a little reserved, chooses to remain far from the madding crowd, enjoys reading in the quiet atmosphere of library, never projects himself to be a popular leader, he is dubbed as an "Introverted" person!

There is nothing wrong or abnormal in being introverted; one does not become a neurotic on that score. It is not at all a negative trait. At the same time, one cannot conclude that all extroverted persons are normal and well-adjusted. Perhaps an extrovert could be a veritable bore, pretty talkative and an irritant, robbing others of their privacy. Strangely enough, an extrovert always receives an undeserving compliment while an introvert is side-lined as a non-social creature!

We must remember that an introverted poet or professor could be a profound scholar in his own chosen discipline, capable of impressing a select gathering with his erudition and common-sense. He may not trumpet his prowess to browbeat others in a public debate. He does not need a "Memory-improvement" course as he might have spent endless hours in the pursuit of his favourite subject. Nor would he make a feverish attempt to enhance his creativity even though he might have done some innovative exercises in his field.

Non-creative people outnumber creative ones in society. One who is obsessed with an irrepressible urge to become famous or outstanding cannot achieve his ambition by a crash course on creativity. An Executive would be a successful leader by allowing freedom to his subordinates to express their views without fear or favour. He would appreciate spontaneity rather than coercive conformity. Such traits are cultivated by repeated exposure to problem-situations. One needs to develop total loyalty to the organization one belongs. Just because an individual does not exhibit creative talents he need not be sunk in despair. He could always work with a creative leader and carry out his ideas expeditiously.

Improvement of memory is not like improving one's biceps with dumb-bells! No fancy quirks or tricks are recommended by Psychologists to enhance memory-power. They concede that by nature some are endowed with a retentive power while some are not blessed with such a capacity. Have not most students memorised their school texts by disciplined study, periodic review and demonstrated their capacity to remember what was taught and learnt? Either out of compulsion to please parents and teachers or out of genuine love for a subject they would have utilised their memory-power to the optimum level. As they ascend to higher levels of education, they tend to procrastinate studies and slacken their serious study-habits. Such an overconfidence and indolence might result in declining memory. Psychologists always advise sustained, systematic study-schedule to maximise memory. They do not prescribe memory-pills! Who knows, in the not-too-distant future, some quacks might introduce pills to improve personality, creativity, integrity and what not!

Psychologists do not claim mystic powers to transform human behaviour overnight. They always advocate, perseverance as well as tolerance to achieve one's goal in life and perhaps a stoic acceptance of one's limitations. Everyone cannot be a Bill Gates; need not become a Narayana Murthy. R.K. Narayan did not become a humorous novelist overnight. Viswanathan Anand might have spent endless hours during his childhood days, playing chess with his mother. Success in life is not a cake-walk! It always involves a good deal of effort coupled with robust optimism. Everyone need not aspire to be a prodigy. One can always lead a quiet, contented life, utilising God-given powers. Psychologists would advocate the philosophy and prayer like" :Oh God! Grant me the tolerance to accept with serenity the things I cannot change, and the courage to change the things I can, and the wisdom to distinguish the two".

> "The soul is plastic and a person who everyday looks upon a beautiful picture, reads a page from some good book, and hears a beautiful piece of music will soon become a transformed person-one born again. — John Ruskin.
>
> "The true teacher like Socrates, plays the part of a midwife."
>
> — *S. Radhakrishnan.*

39

Slow Down Please!

We are constantly bombarded that we are living in space Age — a fast-moving life, where everything has to be accomplished in seconds, if not minutes! At this rate, we might all become robots, remote-controlled or like molecules in an atom, always in a state of perpetual motion! I do not know whether this kind of a super-fast life is beneficial or harmful.

We have kitchen equipment such as micro-wave oven, mixies, grinders, pressure-cookers etc., etc., to lessen the time spent in the kitchen. We have professional obligations - to be in the work-spot precisely on time, parental duties to bathe, feed, dress and transport kids to school as soon as the school-van arrives, rush to the public transport system to reach office on time! Everything seems to be computerised - Information regarding Arrival and Departure of trains and planes, Reservations, waiting list status - with the result we have made life as impersonal as possible! At this rate we would end up reducing ourselves to automatons with remote control arrangements! We would witness in future robots representing different countries, playing chess/Tennis/football and what not! Is it a boon or a bane?

We need to remind ourselves of the aphorism of Henry David Thoreau:

"Nature never makes haste; Her systems revolve at an even pace.:

Look at our Nervous system, Glandular system, Respiratory system, Digestive system.... These cannot be subjected to acceleration, because it requires adequate time to function well. Any attempt to speed up metabolism would only end up in Nervous breakdown! Wisdom warns us of the impending danger of quickening the process.

In her path-breaking book: "How to master change in your life", Mary Carroll Moore lists the benefits of living at a "Slower Pace":

— Slowing down makes me restful inside and gathers my strength.

— If I slow down and pace myself, I will have more energy for whatever life asks me to do.

— Slowing down fills the well of creativity. I get ideas really great when I am not rushing through my days.

— Slowing down is more peaceful. My family likes it when I am more peaceful.

— I am more graceful when I move slower.

— I feel more of the natural abundance of life when I slow down.

— Slowing helps me focus on the moment.

Dr. Ray Rosemann and Dr. Meyer Friedman, two Cardiologists indicated that Coronary-prone people were what they called Type-A personalities: "Driving, Competitive, Obsessive, Aggressive Characters, who are typical workholics, always in a hurry in office or at home or in a restaurant! In contrast to the clock-watching Type A - is the Type - B-person, who is Easy -going, relaxed, ready to take time off to do very little, choosing to walk leisurely than run in rapid strides, who can enjoy good music than watching an Action-movie and who is not really interested in keeping up with Joneses or anyone else!

Don't we wait for ten long months since conception, to deliver a healthy baby? Don't we allow sufficient time in between breakfast and lunch and delay dinner so that proper digestion takes place? Don't we wait for at least three weeks to allow the roofing to stabilise while constructing a house? Did not William Wordsworth take a leisurely walk in the countryside to pen his sonnets, 'Daffodils' and 'Solitary Reaper'? Did not Thomas Gray stray into an abandoned Country Churchyard, to pen his immortal "Elegy"? Did not Thomas Hardy go "far from the madding crowd" to pen his classic novel?

We abandoned the bullock-cart and the soothing, rhythmic sound of jingling bells that adorned the necks of the bullocks as they walked in measured, slow pace! We have forsaken the faster moving horses attached to the carts, with all the rhythmic sounds of the hooves, lending a special majesty and grandeur! Even the chugging sound of the steam locomotives is missing these days because of the diesel and electric engines! We now have the nerve-shattering sound of the jumbo jets piercing through the blue skies, rupturing the ear-drums!

Who would listen to the advice: "Slow-down, please!"

40

What is Creativity?

Why did the Creator create this universe with a bewildering variety of people, each one claiming to be superior over others, thus establishing one's own identity? Some are lean and lanky, while others are short and stocky; some are talkative while others are quite reticent; some are daring and adventurous while others are pretty timid and insecure; some appear smart and intelligent while others are dull and mediocre; some choose to play chess or snooker while others prefer to sweat on a football ground or cricket field; some choose to compose poems while others find it delightful to be a company Executive! Perhaps the creator did not wish to be a factory manager to manufacture a uniform set of human beings. Even though everyone is endowed with sense organs and the nervous system, they tend to differ from one another in their use. The Creator ought to be happy over the variety and novelty of His creations! Like an artist who seldom paints a portrait the same way twice, or a good novelist who seldom describes an incident the same manner twice, the creator also enjoys the variety of His creations. At times he might even be a little unfair and unjust in making some blind or deaf at birth or crippled during infancy. How do we account for this incongruity and partiality? Some are superhuman, some are subhuman, while the vast majority remain simply human. Variety is the spice of life. Novelty has an edge over dull uniformity.

Saint Thyagaraja composed several thousand lyrics during his lifetime on Lord Rama. Each one was tuned to a distinct 'raga' with well-defined ascending and descending scales. Within the framework of a 'raga' each musician has the freedom to display his/her creativity and virtuosity. We do not get bored by listening to the same 'kriti;' sung by several musicians.

Each one bears a stamp of individuality. Though every writer observes the same rules of grammar and syntax how do we account for the distinctive style of writing of Mark Twain, Mahatma Gandhi, Charles Dickens, Bertrand Russell, R.K. Narayan - to cite only a few. Each one is creative in the sense that each one lays individual pathways to excellence. As we read their great works we should not only appreciate the beauty and novelty but strive to evolve a style of our own. Creativity should permeate every teaching-learning situation. Only then would we generate perpetual renewal of talents. We need to remember the maxim 'Innovate or perish.'

The word 'Creativity', in itself, is meaningful. However, we have grown accustomed to offer an explanation and elaboration of an already familiar term. Whatever is novel, unique, unconventional, original is considered creative. To quote Foster:

> "It is like letting down a bucket into the sub-conscious and bringing up things you did not know that you knew, and mixing them with things of ordinary day life that you do know. Out of that mixture you make a work of art. When you have finished it you look at it and wonder how on earth you did it! And indeed you did not do it on earth. It is mysterious.

We get bored with things that remain unchanged for a

long time. Whenever someone introduces a novel idea or product everyone is eager to buy and possess. Teaching remained for a pretty long time a kind of monologue by the preceptors to students. The latter were the recipients and the former, the donors. It occurred to a few creative educators to reverse the trend and make teaching-learning an interactive process. Predictably this resulted in a dynamic interaction wherein both the teacher and the taught were benefitted. But, did it not require rare courage and conviction to break the convention by an invention?

An enterprising psychologist by name B.F. Skinner, an ardent advocate of Operant Conditioning did not stop with his experiments on pigeons and rats. He did display creativity by modifying the classical conditioning of Pavlov with "Instrumental conditioning" or "Operant conditioning". But he became a celebrity by the fabrication of Teaching Machine and Programmed Instruction. At least the average and the below average learners would be grateful to skinner for his contrivance of a gadget that would promote active, self-learning with a built-in feedback system. Whether the initial euphoria of programmed-instruction is still active or extinct, none would dispute the creative idea behind this innovation.

We often extol an eminent scientist or economist or writer as someone endowed with fertile imagination. Imagination lies behind invention, which is a product of creative thinking. Imagination could be Reproductive or Recreative. The former does not provide much scope for creativity, but the latter does. In reproductive imagination an individual merely revives the original experience without any kind of modification. Whereas in recreative imagination the original imagery is transformed into a novel pattern. However, children are mostly imitative or reproductive in their behaviour. They tend to imitate parents and teachers in the acquisition of language and understanding of science. As time passes they do exhibit a kind of inventiveness. Perhaps every learner has to 'per se' pass through a stage of imitation before invention. As Isaac Newton observed:

> "Imitation and invention are the two legs with which the society walks."

The great scientist was humble enough to declare:

> "If I am able to perceive the universe a little more, it is because I have stood on the shoulders of great giants who are my predecessors."

Poets, novelists and artists are endowed with rich imagination and hence their contributions enrich several generations.

Everyone passes through the countryside and most people have their own cares that seldom permit them to stand and stare. But, William Wordsworth, (What an appropriate name) had all the time to stay back and compose a lyric.

> "Behold her, single in the field;
> Yon solitary Highland Lass!
> Reaping and singing by herself;
> Stop here, or gently pass!
> Alone she cuts and binds the grain,
> And sings melancholy strain;
> O listen! for the vale profound
> Is overflowing with the sound"

Are we not familiar with the story of Archimedes? The king of Greece was confronted with a problem. He had ordered a golden Crown to be made. He was not certain whether the goldsmith had used pure gold or some other metal. How to find out was the problem. Meanwhile Archimedes was racking his brains. Always, he was looking for a solution. While eating, sleeping, walking and even while bathing he was brooding over the problem. He was getting into the bath-tub. A good deal of water overflowed when he was getting immersed. Archimedes saw the water splashed all around. That very moment he had a flash: Unmindful of the fact that he was undressed he ran across the street shouting Eureka (which means, "I have found it"). People thought he was mad. But, that genius solved the king's puzzle. There emerges a great scientific truth:

> "When a solid is wholly immersed or partly submerged in a liquid, it experiences an upthrust which is equal to the weight of the liquid it displaces. The weight of the liquid displaced by the submerged part of a body floating in a liquid is equal to the weight of the body."

Though a ship is made of steel, it floats because the upthrust due to displaced water is so large that it is equal to the weight of the ship. What a great creativity! Here is a creative science teacher who composed a poem on the principle of Archimedes:

Eureka!

Archimedes in his bath-tub
Thinking of the king's new crown
Was it gold or baser metal?
On Archy's brow there was a frown.

Gravitation pulled him downward
As the tub began to fill
Buoyant forces lifted upward
Till the tub began to spill

Nearly weightless in the bath-tub
Suddenly he came to see

B less mg the difference
Sink or swim, it is upto me.

Was it gold or plated silver?
No one really knew for sure
But, by dunking in the bath-tub Archy could discern the pure.

Suddenly without his bath-robe
Throughout the streets of Syracuse Naked streaked the great
Olympian A physics legend on the loose!

Novel Population-Control Plan By Twins!

Here is a novel idea of 'Population-control'. Thirty-year old Ambala-born identical twins, Abhay and Ajay Saini hit upon a novel scheme of Population-control. Both are engineers, they married the same day and are fathers of one child each. They identified 35 major problems facing the country and fed them into a computer. Right on the top as the first priority came "Population". So, they worked out a fresh scheme of Population-control, based entirely on incentives. Briefly it is as follows:

A couple who agree to sterilisation after they have one daughter will be entitled to a government bond of Rs. 1.25 lakhs encashable after 21 years. Those who do so after the birth of a son, Rs. 80,000 encashable after 25 years. Those sterilised after two daughters, Rs. 90,000 encashable after 21 years; with two sons, Rs. 30,000/- encashable after 25 years; and those with a son and a daughter Rs. 60,000 encashable in the case of the daughter after 21 years, in the case of the son, after 25 years.

The scheme, if put in operation will initially cost nothing except the cost of printing certificates and be anti-inflationary as the money remains available to the State for over two decades! The Saini brothers have carried out field research on the subject and every peasant or worker they spoke to enthusiastically endorsed it. All it needs now is to be explained to the Prime Minister. That is where the buck stops!

41

Innovate or Perish

It has often baffled the common man how some people become uncommon. We label such extraordinary individuals as prodigies or creatives. What is it that differentiates them from the non-creatives?

We seldom realise that we owe our success or failure in life to our parents who influence us a great deal in our formative years. Fortunate are those blessed with parents who would listen, appreciate differences, encourage risk-taking and discourage blind conformity.

Are we to believe that some are born creative? If so, can we disregard environmental stimulation altogether? Psychologists do not subscribe to this deterministic or fatalistic view. While we do come across a few instances of precocity at an early age, most creatives are self-made.

For instance, what kind of an environment did the famous inventor Thomas Alva Edison have? When his teacher labelled Edison an addled boy, his mother became furious and withdrew him from school. She groomed him at home. The rest is history.

Bertrand Russell had a private tutor at home during his childhood. Institutionalised education aims at a kind of standardisation that kills initiative and innovation. Unlucky are those whose teachers encourage memorisation and verbatim reproduction as the "summum bonum" of education. Stereotyping is antithetical to progress. A society that promotes and encourages conformity, remains stagnant forever. It might even perish.

Here are a few suggestions to parents and teachers:

— Encourage articulation even if it sounds eccentric or ludicrous.

— Resist the temptation to advise unless it is sought.

— Do not snub or ridicule for mistakes.

— Do not give wrong explanations when their questions baffle you.

— Do not discipline too much, fixing specific hours for homework.

— Do not get upset over progress reports. Children resent harsh criticisms.

— Allow children to be autonomous. Do not breathe down their necks.

— Build a small library at home and let the children start collecting books with their pocket-money.

— Narrate biographies of eminent persons who have been able to achieve a great deal.

— Do not compare brothers and sisters. It would hurt them.

— Provide opportunities for outings during week-ends and holidays. Let them write whatever they see.

— Allow a child to be a child.

42

Why Nip the Early Blossom?

Way back in 1975, the first ever World Conference for Gifted children was held in the Royal College of Surgeons, London. About 500 delegates from 50 countries, representing Government Departments, specifically dealing with the needs of the Gifted and also some Professors conducting Research in this area attended the conference.

From the U.S. Office of Education, the Director of Education for the Gifted and Talented, Dr. Harold C. Lyon. Jr. participated and made some significant observations. The title of the article is drawn from his comments.

Dr. Lyon used to walk down to his office in Washington D.C. from his apartment, located just a few blocks away, instead of availing the limousine services made available. It was only to escape the tension with the clogging of cars and trucks. He would walk back home in the evening too so that he could reflect over the day's work and plan for the following day. Very few Americans enjoy this luxury!

It was the spring season. One morning, on his way to office, Dr. Lyon noticed several thousand tulips in the National Park - a gift from the Netherlands! It was a glorious sight indeed! They were beginning to blossom in a race for glory with the cherry blossoms. Dr. Lyon noticed some 10 to 15 tulips blosomming a little ahead of the rest, raising their heads majestically!

It lingered in his vision even after he reached his office. As he was returning home in the evening he noticed the gardener in the Park, literally amidst the tulip bed, clipping off the early bloomers so as to maintain uniformity! It disturbed him a great deal.

At the same time it set him thinking about the shoddy treatment of the early blooming talented and gifted youth. Very often they have their "blossoms clipped" in class by unimaginative teachers who were obsessed with standardised instruction and evaluation. Neither the teacher nor the student had time to stand and stare at things and events beyond the class.

Even in a progressive country like the U.S., not all the Benjamin Franklyns, the Alexander Flemings and the Graham Bells receive the special attention they need! Everyone has to fall in line with the majority and march like soldiers. The egalitarian tendency deeply entrenched in us, sometimes makes us blind to the reality of glaring individual differences. About our country, the less said, the better. With the student-population steadily on the increase, exceeding the plinth area available in the classroom, which again is compounded by demotivated teachers, where is the time to spot the early blossoms?

'Many a gem of purest serene' in our classrooms—a Ramanujan, a Raman and a Rabindranath Tagore - remain in obscurity until some day their dazzling intellect stun the world and arrest attention.

Recently Prof. Amartya Sen won the Nobel Prize in Welfare Economics for his work done some two decades ago on Poverty and famine. He had his early education at Shatiniketan, where he was born.

It was Tagore who christened him with the name 'Amartya'. Gurudev said, "I have given him a name which is not very common. Be careful with the spelling, or its meaning will change." What a prophecy by the 'illustrious poet'! Some six decades later, Amartya lived upto his name and won the Nobel Prize. He is in the company of the great soul who named him. Has the ambience at Shantiniketan sowed the seed of greatness that sprouted matured and blosommed ultimately? The gifted should not be left in wilderness.

What is it that a gifted child needs from society? They need an opportunity for free expression, not suppression. We do not know whether Ramanujan's Teacher at Town High School, Kumbakonam could match the brilliance of his student! Raman's Professor in Presidency College, Madras, could not answer the teen-ager-prodigy's question.'

Of course, later Raman himself, found an answer, to his 'question'. R.K. Narayan's teacher in Maharaja's College, Mysore taught him several texts and novels and almost all the rules of grammar found in the book of Wren and Martin'. But the student outsmarted his teacher with the gift of his pen!

A nuclear physicist was giving a special lecture to a group of 26 children, aged seven to eleven, attending a one-week residential course in Canada. The learned scientist said: "To make electricity you need a lot of heat. In a nuclear power station we take a mass of uranium and fire into it a neutron - the smallest known particle!"

"Oh No! It isn't! Until recently a neutron was believed to be the smallest known particle, but now the neutrino, a particle of antimatter is believed to be the smallest known", said an eight year old! The scientist smiled and acknowledged the observation of the gifted.

Give your children a chance to talk about their hobbies and when they surprise you by their command of vocabulary of their hobbies recognise the fact that you have been offering an unduly calorie-free teaching diet!

Let us agree to cease to underestimate, underchallenge and undernourish our children. Let us not deny some children their intellectual and academic birth-right.

Teachers of bygone days had an uncanny insight into the gem of giftedness lurking in some young minds in the class. They found time to talk to them beyond the class-hours.

All that is expected of teachers of gifted children is absolute sincerity and candour to admit ignorance in areas where they are not sufficiently well-informed and allow the precocity of the learner to surface.

They need an inexhaustible reservoir of energy and enthusiasm to run along with their students in the pursuit of excellence, though the youth are far ahead in thinking and imagination.

Above all, they have to have an uncompromising stand on discipline and hard work, because, achievement in any field is not a cake-walk!

It is a myth to say that the gifted can take care of themselves. They also need a "Guru". Ekalavya could outsmart Arjuna in archery, because of his total devotion to Dronacharya.

After heaping glory after glory in life, Sir Isaac Newton had the humility to declare that he could perceive the Universe a little clearer because he was perched on the shoulders of giants who were his predecessors!

All toppers in examinations are not necessarily gifted! All the gifted need not be toppers in examinations. But, they do reach top positions in life. However, they never kick off the ladders—their primary school teachers—upon whose shoulders they climbed, to view the world!

43

Better Light A Candle...

It was the end of October, 1961. Winter was just setting in New York City, the most impersonal city in the World! Teachers' College, Columbia, was housed in its old 19th century building, not too far from Harlem, the dreaded place where the low-income group Negroes are concentrated. Adjoining the college stands the old dormitory, Whittier Hall, where students are accommodated. I checked in, feeling most uncomfortable in that blessed city where food (vegetarian), climate, education and entertainment would pose problems to the meek and weak-hearted'. The next day an American arrived with his baggage to occupy the room opposite mine. I was hesitant to address the newcomer. I heard the knock and when I opened the door of my room, the newcomer, Jim Velarius, an white man, stepped in, shook hands with me and spent nearly an hour, enquiring my background (an East-West Centre Scholar from Madras, enrolled for Advanced Education course at the University of Hawaii). I was in Columbia for a semester. Within an hour, acquaintance became close friendship when Jim related his background and his motivation to join Columbia Teachers' College.

Jim graduated in Science from the University of Illinois, Chicago, got a job as an Executive in one of the foremost Departmental Stores, having a chain of establishments from California to New York. Jim could fly any airline any time, stay in posh hotels, visit any of the branches of Woolworth, Departmental stores and furnish reports to the Head Office. He was literally floating in dollars for a couple of years, still a bachelor at 30.

On a wintry day at Detroit, Jim was about to step into Woolworth on his work. Just then an yellow mini-bus brought a bunch of little children, accompanied by a lady teacher. There was something odd about the appearance of those kids, who were entering the Ford Museum, to enjoy viewing the models of cars, made ever since Henry Ford designed his first four-wheeler to the latest design. Jim forgot his duty, approached the elderly lady and enquired about those kids. He was informed that they were all mentally retarded children on a field-trip. Jim was moved beyond expression. He lost no time in surveying the Catalogues of Universities that offered a course in Teaching the Mentally Retarded and chose Columbia for studies. He chose to discard a job that gave him all the comforts that one could aspire for in life and prefer a path that only a person with a missionary zeal would opt for. This is only to state that not all Americans are after dollars and luxury. They choose a vocation that would afford fulfilment. Upon completion of the course, Jim joined as a teacher in a School for the Mentally Retarded about 160 km away from the din and bustle of 'New York City'. He was earning one-fourth of what he grossed at Woolworth, but his satisfaction multiplied fourfold!

In a world designed for the able and the ablest, the disabled find themselves misfits, discarded and detached. The mentally retarded are exceptional children, who cannot, for obvious reasons, profit from the kind of instruction carried on in conventional classes because of cognitive deficit. They do not, on that score, forfeit their right to lead a fruitful life in tune with whatever limited potentialities they possess. It is not their fault to be born handicapped mentally as it can be traced back to their genetic background. It may be due to chromosomal abnormalities or because of anaesthetic drugs consumed by pregnant mothers to reduce the discomfort during delivery. The toxic substances pass through the placenta, enter the blood stream of the foetus, reduce the available oxygen and affect the child's Central Nervous System. Though these infants appear healthy at birth, they frequently show relatively little spontaneous motor activity, slow heart and respiration rates and poor circulation.

Sometimes emotional reaction during pregnancy too might result in the birth of a mentally retarded child. Pregnant women respond to emotions such as rage or anxiety with a massive outpouring of adrenal hormones. These secretions may enter the foetus's blood-stream. The movements of the foetus due to adrenalin increase abnormally which could result later in irritability, cleft palate and subnormal intellect.

In olden days the mentally deficient were labelled rather contemptuously as Idiots, Imbeciles and Morons. With the advent of modern Psycho-pathology they are termed Mild, Moderate, Severe and Profound Retarded children. The "mild" ones are educable while the "moderate" ones are trainable in schools specially designed to meet their needs. The remaining two categories—severe and profound retardates—need custodial care all through their lives as they cannot profit from any kind of education.

The mildly retarded and the moderately retarded ones are not taught just the three R's as we do with normal ones. Rather, they are imparted three A's, namely, Personal Adequacy, Social Adequacy and Occupational Adequacy. Teachers, by and large, are accustomed to good feedback from children they teach, which, in turn, boosts their self-image and importance. In the case of the mentally retarded we need a different set of traits for teachers who can bestow care upon children- who might remain unresponsive and even frustrate teachers who attempt to influence them. The curriculum for the mildly retarded who are educable, should be restructured, simplified, slow-paced, individualized and non-competitive. A good deal of empathy and warmth on the part of the teacher is required to make these children repose trust upon them and love to respond.

The modernately retarded are trainable to acquire simple skills that would prepare them to become economically independent. They cannot aspire to rise to the level of the milder ones, to acquire knowledge. Under supervision and constant guidance they can be trained to lead a life of satisfactory adjustment. Parents need education to handle such children. They should not compare such children with their normal ones and cause depression to themselves as well as to their children. Acceptance, adjustment and adaptation are required to deal with these kids. Early' diagnosis by trained psychologists or psychiatrists could save valuable time for appropriate intervention programme.

In countries like Denmark, Sweden, the United Kingdom and the USA, the needs of the retarded children receive a good deal of attention from the Government. The impetus to educate such children actually originated from two French Medical Doctors, ITARD and SEGUIN and an Italian Doctor, Montessori. The trio devoted all their energies to brighten the lives of those who remained in obscurity. The tenacity and conviction with which these 19th Century educators transformed the lives of the less able cannot be so easily assessed and acknowledged. They followed the dictum:

> It is better to light a candle
> than curse the darkness".

44

Increasing Pupil-Strength, Decreasing Teacher Strength

As the strength of the classroom increases, teacher's strength to teach decreases. Of late one witnesses a boom or demand for formal education in formal schools and colleges. The classroom that accommodated about forty or fifty has to cater to the needs of double or even more. With inadequate furniture or even plinth area a teacher looks at a sea of faces and gasps for breath. However much he raises his voice it hardly reaches beyond three rows. How could we blame the students for their inattentiveness or indifference? What right do we have to accuse the teacher for his/her inability to pay individual attention? It is a kind of mass-feeding that would naturally end in a mess. It has not occurred to the educational planners to take stock of the prevailing chaos in classroom and work out a viable solution to the vexatious issue. Perhaps the day is not far off when we may have to admit students who will have to stand and learn similar to the standing passengers in an overcrowded bus! Whether we like it or not we cannot possibly arrest the "drop-in rate", and we attempt all possible means of retaining those who have opted to join formal schools.

Let us attempt to find a way out of the impasse. All educational institutions should work in two shifts of four-hour duration with two sets of teaching faculty and students. The first shift could commence at 8 a.m and close at 12 noon and the second shift could assemble at 1 p.m and work till five-o-clock in the evening. Such an arrangement would ease the burden of teachers as well as the taught. It is not necessary to provide a recess. A few minutes' break between classes would suffice. The time-table should be so framed as to provide each class/section exclusively for library work. At all levels of schooling, library should be the hub of scholastic work. Knowledge is expanding so fast that a teacher, howsoever well informed, cannot clear the doubts of students. But, students could be guided to refer the sources from which requisite details are obtainable. Instead of feeding students with a standardised textbook-based knowledge teachers could instil in inquisitive learners real thirst for self-learning.

260 books are produced each second! Placed side by side and cover to cover, the books printed in a year alone would circle the earth four times!

Instruction in classes should be restricted to the minimum, thereby affording students opportunity for interactive learning. Teachers should be facilitators, for self-learning than dictators of prefabricated notes! In every class, a teacher is likely to come across a few bright students who could outsmart the teacher. This should not disturb the teacher's ego. Rather, it should remind him to be a life-long learner. While we remember Raman and Ramanujan we seldom remember their teachers! Perhaps they functioned as ladders by climbing which these prodigies could perceive the universe better!

45

Agony and Ecstasy in Research

Research is undoubtedly a good exercise for everyone to sharpen his intellect, devise an appropriate tool of measurement and carry out the investigation in accordance with a carefully planned research design. It calls for simple, direct, but effective presentation of the procedures employed by the researcher and the inferences drawn from the study. It should be possible for another research worker to replicate the work and verify whether a similar study would yield the same results.

With these prefacing remarks, let us consider the case of educational research. It is trailing far behind similar work in other areas, judging by the number of Ph.D theses that have been submitted in any university in India. If research "per se" is really a noteworthy endeavour, why should educational research lag behind? The answer to this question can be found only when a research scholar is frank enough to admit, without fear or favour, the hurdles he had to cross before gaining Ph.D.

The most important need for a research worker is a competent guide who can make the student think for himself. Guidance does not mean merely leading a docile scholar along a path best known only to the guide, so as to reach a predetermined destination. On the other hand it should be an exhilarating experience for the novice to initiate, clear the path and forge ahead under the able guidance of a sincere and hardworking guide. In this process both the guide and the student learn something new. There might be occasions when the student would feel lost and become desperate. Under such circumstances, it is the duty of the guide to cheer up the student.

Secondly, the research worker must be provided the optimum facilities to carry out his research project.

Since much of educational research involves a good deal of field-work, the agencies concerned must extend maximum cooperation. For instance, if a study were to involve administration of a test or questionnaire to the students in schools, the heads of institutions should not look upon the research scholar as an intruder into the regular routine of the school system. Of course, it is also necessary for the research scholar to write in advance or probably visit the school to fix up a mutually convenient date and time for administering the test. The class teacher has to lend a helping hand. It is too much to expect the pupils to appreciate the value of an educational research and cooperate spontaneously. When pandemonium prevailed in the class at the time of test-administration, the research scholar would be fed up with rigorous procedures outlined in the experimental design and only aim at the completion of work somehow or other. The data obtained under such conditions might vitiate the research work and the findings might be unreliable.

Another important factor contributing to the development of educational research is the application of research findings in classroom teaching and school organisation. Even though a few researches may be of a fundamental nature, contributing to the development of educational theory, the bulk of educational research is of an applied nature.

If a research work is conducted to establish the validity of a guidance programme to tackle the problem of underachievement in schools, school authorities as well as the Department of Education must take it on a priority basis and train teachers in some of the elementary techniques of guidance and counselling. In the absence of such a follow-up programme, an ardent research worker is compelled to conclude that, after all, his labour, apart from procuring a Ph.D, was only an exercise in futility. Unfortunately in our country, educational innovations and practice rarely stem from educational research!

Let not the above argument be misconstrued as a note of despondency and dissuade the scholars from the pursuit of research. The hurdles are not altogether insurmountable. Perhaps, educational research under such adverse conditions might help the investigator to develop diplomacy, tact, resourcefulness and above all, patience, in dealing with a variety of agencies. This, in itself, is an educative experience. When the researcher reaches the goal he forgets the agony and what remains is only an ecstasy!

> "We always like those who admire us but we don't always like those we admire".
>
> — *La Roche-Foucauld.*

46

Teach Thyself...

Our task as teachers does not end merely with imparting knowledge. We need to ensure that students absorb, retain and recall later what they learnt in class. It is common knowledge that learning become easier and more long-lasting when students are deeply interested.

There is an in-built resistance or reluctance among students to any kind of testing. Because, it exposes their deficiencies and makes them feel guilty when they receive poor grades. There is always an element of anxiety whenever students have to take a test.

An attempt was made by the writer in a College of Education during a Psychology class. A day before the test, four questions were dictated to students from the unit of instruction. The students were informed that any one of the four questions - to be decided by drawing lots - will have to be answered by everyone.

Initially the students were jubilant because the questions were leaked out by the teacher and hence they could be pretty sure of what they should do. Only a little later could they perceive the catch. Which among the four questions is likely to be picked up by the teacher? Even granting that no foul-play is attempted, the chance of every question is just one-fourth in terms of probability. Should they gamble and prepare thoroughly for one or two? Supposing the question does not figure in the test what will be their predicament?

After debating over these issues, students were left with no choice but to prepare themselves to answer all the four questions. The teacher's intention was only to make them read the entire unit and not resort to elimination. But, he cleverly concealed it by a concession that was only a ruse.

A surprise was in store for students the following day. Everyone kept wondering which question would be picked up by the teacher.

Their motivation was writ large upon their faces. Teachers always enjoy the prerogative of changing the rules of the game, particularly when no malafide motives are intended.

The students were seated in six rows of ten each in a class with a strength of 60. Commencing from the left in the front row, everyone was asked to call out the numbers 'one', 'two', 'three' and 'four' and repeat the same till the last person called out 'four'. They were still is a quandary as to why the teacher asked them to perform this exercise without breaking the suspense of picking out the question for the test. The teacher then announced that all students who called out number 'one' would answer the first question, 'two' the second one, 'three' the third one and 'four' the fourth question.

Since four students seated in a row answered four different questions, there was no scope for cheating. The teacher was relieved of invigilation. As a matter of fact, a good deal of enthusiasm was evident and each one was busy answering. They were instructed to write about a page within just fifteen minutes. A bigger surprise awaited them.

While the students were writing, the teacher prepared bits of papers for evaluation. When they finished answering, the teacher collected their answer-papers and distributed to each student a slip of paper. They were asked to write on the slip "Inter-evaluation". The answer papers were distributed at random. It was ensured that no one received his/her paper. The were asked to write on the evaluation slip the name of the student whose answer book was given for evaluation. They were asked to read the answers twice carefully and then award a score out of ten. They were also free to write suggestors and comments for improvement.

Soon after the evaluation was completed the teacher collected all the answer books and the evaluation slips. Students were given fresh slips of paper and asked to write on the top 'self-evaluation'. Each one received his/her answer book for evaluation. They were asked to go through their answers and award a score. Their names also were recorded in their evaluation slips.

The teacher collected the answer books and evaluation slips. The entire exercise lasted just one class-hour and the students were really ecstatic over the novel method of testing and evaluation.

The teacher evaluated each script and entered the score in another slip, referred to as 'Teacher-evaluation'. Now the teacher had three sets of independent evaluations. There was a significant positive correlation between the teacher's evaluation and Inter-evaluation. The correlation between students' self-evaluation and Inter-evaluation was positive but not significant. Similarly the teacher-evaluation and self-evaluation also yielded non-significant positive correlation.

If only teachers could be creative and open-minded, it would be possible to make tests enjoyable.

47

When a Degree Expires...

Knowledge is an ever-flowing stream; it is not a stagnant pool. Everyone has the opportunity to acquire knowledge and wisdom from schools and colleges during the formative years. Does the process of learning cease when an individual receives a degree in a convocation? Can we arrest the momentum and halt the activity?

One of the factors contributing to the obsolescence of a University Degree or even a string of degrees obtained by our learned professors in the Teaching Profession is a sense of complacency. It breeds mediocrity and a kind of passivity. Can the teacher become role-models to students if they stop replenishing the stock of ideas gathered as students way back? The astronomical increment of knowledge in every field of human endeavour is so awesome that one has to update periodically so as to arrest fossilisation.

When we buy torch-cells in the shop we find the expiry dates printed on them. It means that beyond that date it ceases to have the power of illumination. In a chemist's shop we look into the expiry dates of a tonic or capsule. Beyond those dates the potency of the medicine wanes and disappears. We need to apply the same yardstick to the acquisition of university degrees. Why shouldn't our university authorities print in the degrees and diplomas they confer the expiry dates of knowledge as well, so that it would remind the holders of degrees to renew them, much as we renew a driving licence to drive an automobile!

We need to incorporate into our system of college teaching as well as teaching in schools, a sabbatical leave so that each faculty number would be required to undergo a specially designed refresher course in their respective disciplines. We also need a training institution engaged in the task of providing such advanced knowledge and information. Adequate care must be bestowed in staffing such an institution so that it does not become another 'good old grind'!

Faculty members of proven merit and capabilities drawn from the National Laboratories and Research centres could be hired on contract basis for such a catalysis.

Attendance for these courses should be long enough to gain and consolidate knowledge. Project-work and field-study ought to form part of the curriculum. The participants must get back to teaching with renewed zest. Since the training has to be interactive with a good deal of feedback, the number of participants should not exceed twenty. The duration of training also should be for a minimum of twelve weeks.

The programmes offered at the Academic Staff colleges under the U.G.C. are not adequate to instil the requisite skills in learning and teaching. It gets filled with too many lectures, too little of follow-up and almost nothing in terms of output by participants. Of course, everyone receives a nice certificate for having undergone the training.

In the absence of creating such a healthy and effective training programme, teaching standards in colleges and universities may not improve at all. Rather it would proceed in reverse gear! The capacity for self-renewal and growth of the human brain is enormous. Let us exploit to the maximum instead of allowing atrophy to set in.

48

Teaching and Research-Complementary or Contradictory?

Education is a flowing stream, not a stagnant pool. Everyone engaged in the business of teaching needs to update knowledge through constnat review and revision so as to check obsolescence. Gone are the days when the teacher would stand on a raised platform to pontificate or teach in a commanding tone that would keep all students in a state of rapt attention. The awe-inspring figure of the teacher would make students more or less mute spectators. It would be all the more accentuated in a class wherein majority of students are less fluent in English than in their mother-tongue. Would such a climate be conducive to stimulate independent thinking among students?

We do not know when a swift turnaround took place, transforming classroom-climate. Teaching and learning are inextricably interwoven. The proof of lasting learning is a kind of flexibility of the thinking process. Neither the Pythogorean theorem nor the Theory of Relativity can be fully grasped by students unless they are provoked to cite instances from day-to-day life. Verbatim reproduction of an elegant definition given in Textbooks is not an indicator of knowledge-assimilation. What worked in section -A- of a class might fail miserably with Section -B-, when the former consists of above-average learners and the latter is full of the below-average. Unless a teacher has a resilient mind to adapt instruction to the learner-capability, he cannot be called an effective teacher.

Experience equals the capacity to teach, multiplied by the desire to teach, multiplied by the years of service. A zero somewhere in that equation would give one consequential results.

Every teacher is a researcher in the broad sense of the term. In other words he re-searches again and again, year after year, alternate strategies of teaching the same subject. Every such search leads to a new dimension, a new perspective. Research should not be viewed in a narrow way as something done in a laboratory by erudite scholars, to be published in a journal or budding scholars, to be submitted to obtain a research degree!

A creative teacher does not merely go by the standard exercises given in the textbook. He improvises. Why not ask students in class VI, to frame questions similar to those found in the textbook? Would it not be a pleasant pastime to ask students to give a list of words with similar spelling but dissimilar pronunciation! e.g. Poor -Door; Heal-Hear; Love-Rose; Care-Cane.

A research-minded teacher finds it delightful to be innovative in classroom-teaching. He/She need not be always obsessed with rigorous Research-methodology and Statistical analysis. As a matter of fact, one who boasts of his/her Ph.D may not always be an effective classroom teacher. His communication may be pedantic and loaded. On the other hand, there are teachers who can keep a class spell-bound with a simple pendulum experiment by associating it with a swing found in the country-side trees. You can tie a longer rope and a shorter one, side by side, to demonstrate the difference in oscillation.

Teachers, in general, think that teaching History is a mere narration of events. A research-minded teacher can enliven the class thus: He can ask a student to play the role of Akbar, another the role of Ashoka and the third one to be Aurangazeb. Let them have a debate on "Religion". What would be the contribution of each? Supposing Robert Clive had lost the Battle of Plassey, what would be the consequences? This can make students think in uncommon ways?

Education is a way of triggering the thinking process. Are not good teachers equally good in a kind of research that would make them better teachers?

> "Man biologically considered, is the most formidable of all the beasts of prey and indeed the only one that preys systematically on its own species."
>
> —*William James.*

> "Worry is interest paid on trouble before it becomes due".
>
> — *Inge*

49

The Rise and Fall of the Titanic...

Seldom do we get an opportunity to witness the rapid rise and the precipitous fall of a citadel of learning, a Juggernaut of National Eminence-the National Council of Educational Research and Training (NCERT) New Delhi! At times the incredible does take place, leaving the loyalists agape and aghast! We need Titan watches for citizens and also a Titanic reform in Education for the country's progress!

For several decades during the 20th century it was believed that a high school teacher could be trained in about nine months with a judicious mix of Psychology, Philosophy, School Administration and Teaching methodology. The premier institution in South India was Teachers college, Saidapet at Madras. Teachers of repute received rudimentary knowledge of teaching at this holy institution. Later came up Meston Training College, Royapettah in Madras.

Affiliated to the University of Madras, one of the oldest universities, these colleges awarded the degree of L.T. to start with and later changed it to B.T. None gate-crashed for admission and therefore, the gates were kept open to all those who desired to learn to teach. Old students of this great institution during pre-Independence days, still recall with nostalgia the illustrious preceptors who groomed them for the noblest of profession.

Somewhere in the early fifties, the nascent Annamalai University opened a Teacher-education section and awarded B.Ed Degree (Sounds better than B.T!). Since all those who joined colleges of Education were really imbued with an intrinsic, irrespressible urge to mould young minds, they seldom minded the poor monetary compensation they received. Even in those days every other profession proved to be more lucrative than the profession of teaching! In course of time, demand outstripped supply.

More teachers were needed for the emerging schools and the teeming millions craving for schooling. More Teacher-training Institutions sprang up. Even advanced level courses -M.Ed-were introduced although it was not the felt need. Some of the old, reputed professors of the traditional Teachers' College had real mastery over education even though they did not acquire the M.Ed Degree!

In the early Sixties a national awakening arose to revitalise 'Teacher-education'. The Ministry of Education, Government of India set up an autonomous body called the National Council of Educational Research and Training (NCERT) at New Delhi. It was felt and rightly so that the preparation of an ideal teacher has to be on an extended time-frame than mere nine months. Just as an engineer or a doctor goes through a 4-year course, a teacher also needs a 4-year course of education.

Certainly it sounded radical because, one-year Teacher-education was an accepted pattern for a pretty long time. The NCERT meant business. It sought collaboration with the Ohio State University, Colombus, Ohio, USA, to evolve a new 4-year Integrated Programme of Teacher-education. Several Indian educationists were selected and sent to the

US to receive short-term training in this regard. Consultants from the US also came over to India to stay, establish and stablise the Colleges of Education.

On August 1, 1963, the Regional College of Education, Mysore was inaugurated by (late) Sardar K.M. Panikkar, Vice-chancellor of Mysore University. Similar Colleges of Education were also set up at Ajmer, Bhopal and Bhubaneswar. The college at Mysore catered to the needs of the four Southern States and the Union Territory of Pondicherry. The buildings were still under construction. It was on August 7, 1965, that (late) Sri. M.C. Chagla, Union Minister for Education visited the Regional College of Education, Mysore, to declare open the new buildings. Delivering the Inaugural Address, the learned Jurist observed:

> "The modern idea is that a teacher must know as much of the subject that he is teaching as the methods of teaching, and therefore this 4-year Integrated course is a tremendous improvement in Teacher-training. Our idea is to have similar courses in several universities during the Fourth-Five-Year Plan."

A phenomenal growth took place on the campus during the sixties and the seventies when we had Miss. Ahalya Chari (now with the Krishnamoorthy foundation, Madras) as the Principal.

The cream of the student-community from all over South India converged upon the campus to become specialists in teaching Science, Commerce, English and Technology. The college also offered courses of One-year duration in Home-science, Agriculture, Mathematics, Science and English. To meet the needs of Higher Secondary Courses, M.Sc. Ed., courses in Chemistry, Physics and Mathematics were also opened, bringing students from all over the country. Well qualified faculty members drawn from all over India interacted with students all the time. Several hostels were built to accommodate girls and boys who opted for the college soon after their higher-secondary education.

The writer recalls with nostalgia the memorable occasions during his three-decade service when he struggled to answer several questions raised by smart students. Seldom does a teacher acknowledge the debt he owes to his students for his cognitive growth and development! The students who passed out of the Regional College of Education were welcomed and absorbed in Central Schools and other reputed Public Schools. Indeed they exuded confidence and competence in handling classes. I am sure all those who read this article, who had the privilege of spending their four formative years in the Regional College of Education, would reflect and retrospect over their delectable days.

One of the mysteries of life is disillusionment with a constructive design. Questions were raised in the Parliament and also within the Ministry of Human Resources Development regarding its economic feasibility.

Can we afford this costly experimentation in education! Should we continue or discontinue? Why shouldn't we run Inservice Programmes for teachers in schools than running regular courses? Such queries were raised.

The Titanic could not withstand the tidal waves of the sceptics. Priorities were revised. The college metamorphosed into the Regional Institutes of Education. It is an unbelievable shadow of the magnificent stature that it once had!

50

What a Paradigm Shift in Schooling!

Over the past five decades since Independence there has been a phenomenal growth of schools of all kinds in our country to -cater to the growing needs of the unchecked growth of population. Still, most classrooms are bursting at the seams as we struggle to accommodate much more than we did earlier. The net result is a kind of total impersonality whereby a teacher finds it quite difficult to recognise his own students in the market place. The only identification that comes to his rescue is the school uniform. The teacher would ask: "Are yo studying in ..... school?" The boy would reply, "yes Sir! I am in your class Sir. My name is...." we can't blame the teacher.

Can there be anything more funny than what is stated above? I shudder to think of the years ahead with more and more students seeking admission and more and more inadequate space for accommodation. It is not just the provision of physical accommodation, but mental adjustment or adaptation that is needed for the teacher as well as the taught. Imagine for a moment a class teacher of seventh standard struggling to teach seventy or eighty students in a class. However bold his writing on the black-board might be students beyond the fifth row would find it impossible to perceive! The vocal chords of the techer must be widened and activated to the limit so that he is heard by the back-benchers. There would always be a scramble for the front rows. In all fairness boys would condescend to leave it to the fair sex. Among the girls whoever occupied these rows on the first day would claim them as though they were reserved accommodation!

Whenever a teacher tries to raise his voice beyond a respectable limit, his brain would not function as it should! Instead of teaching he should be actually shouting!

Such a classroom set-up would be a haven for many mischief-mongers because it is difficult to spot them in the crowd. The more, the merrier, perhaps!

There cannot be anything more fracical than conducting a test in such a class unless the teahcer is hydra-headed, with multi-dimensional vision to detect copy writers!

Just as corruption has become more or less an unavoidable adjunct to everyday life, copying has become so pervasive that no headmaster would entertain any complaint from any teacher. Having been accustomed to such a "no-holds-bared" environemnt, it should be irksome for our students to write public examination under strict, vigilant supervision. Can there be anything more disgraceful than seeking Police protection to conduct public examination in school? Ten long years of schooling have failed to inculcate in our students fairness and honesty. What a paradigm shift! Can we call these schools educational institutions? Have we redefined the term 'Education' to mean a license' to do what one wishes to do? Do we, in colleges of education, have to advise the Teacher-trainees to bestow' individual attention when it is impossible to pay even collective attention in such a mass-congregation? Why do we perpetuate the gulf between precept and practice?

Against such a horrifying spectacle, septuagenarians couldn't help comparing and contrasting their good old school days with the current ones. Never in the past a class-strength exceeded forty. Often it would be around thirty only. No studnet could escape the notice of the teacher. The teacher would remember not only the names of every student but also their whole family background. Many from the same family would have attended the same school. Teacher would know the strength as well as shortcomings of every student and would never hesitate to pull them up whenever they lagged behind! Copying was considered a cognizable offence, leading to dismissal or detention. Never in the past any headmaster felt compelled to seek police bandobast to conduct public examination. Let us face it. Are we progressing or regressing in this new cliche of PARADIGM SHIFT?

51

National Imperatives

DESTINY of the nation is being shaped in classroom! What a prophetic observation by the Education Commission (1964)! Half-a-century in the history of a Nation is neither too short nor too long! It is quite adequate and good enough to consolidate the best and eradicate the 'not-so-good'!

Nearly a decade and a half after Independence in the early Sixties, it occurred to the then Ministry of Education (renamed Human Resources Development)_ to set up an autonomous body called the National Council of Educational Research and Training (NCERT) in New Delhi, to plan formulate and execute innovation in Education, particularly in the area of Teacher Education.

Several eminent educationists like Raja Roy Singh, Prem Kripal, Rais Ahmed, S.V.C. Ayya, Chandra Kanth—to name only a few — could be called the "Pilgrim fathers" to lead the contry's premier Education Agency in a healthy direction. Occupying a wing of the Ministry adjacent to the WHO office in New Delhi, the experts went about recruiting personnel form all over India to help usher in a vibrant, viable Teacher Education Programme for the country. It was their aim to rouse the pedagogues from their somnolence and complacency and visualise a path-breaking Programme of Teacher-Education. The launching pad was very firm—

no financial crunch, no dearth of talents and no paucity of motivation and commitment.

Ecducational experts from the Ohio State University, Columbus, USA, were invited to design a four-year Integrated Programme of Teacher-education. Till then, the country had only one-year training Programme for graudates. These Colleges of Education had about seven or eight Faculty Members. The student-strength seldom exceeded a hundred. It was felt, and rightly so, that professional preparation for Teaching needs an extended training period and the prospective applicants need to be admitted soon after their completion of Secondary Education. The primary objective was to catch them young, inculcate right attitudes, provide strong foundation in basic disciplines and integrate the content with teaching mthodology so as to make College of Education a comprehensive educational complex.

To bring together faculty members representing disciplines such as Chemistry, Physics, Biology, Mathematics Regional Languages, Engish, Commerce, Technology Agriculture, Physical Education, Arts and Crafts was something unheard of in our country. The whole country was divided into four zones, with Ajmer, Bhopal, Bhubaneswar and Mysore being chosen to establish Regional Colleges of Educaton. These were supposed to run the innovative 4-year Integrated coures as well as the conventional One-year Course in Teacher-education.

Most of the Faculty members who had the unique privilege of participating in this educational experimentation look back with pride and pleasure the exciting interaction among themselves and also the challenging encounters with bright youngsters in classrooms. The products of these 4-year courses were in great demand. Kendriya Vidyalayas, Public Schools and reputed Private Schools absorbed these teachers since they found their content-competency and teaching methodology far superior to that of the existing one-year trained graduates.

Later, Post-graduate courses in Techer-education with specialisation in disciplines such as Physics, Mathematics, Chemistry and Life Sciences were introduced to prepare teachers for Higher Secondary Schools. These courses were open to students form all over India. Faculty members from Universities readily came forward to participate in this unique endeavour. This proved to be an additional feather to the cap. Products of these courses had no difficulty in securing placement. Quite a few of them even joined prestigious Research Institutions like, the Tata Institute of Fundamental Research (TIFR) Council of Scientific and Industrial Research (CSIR) and also institutions in the USA.

Any educational scheme, if properly conceived and prudently pursued and proved useful too, ought to be continued with unrelenting faith and vigour. Considering the benefits that accrue to the Nation in terms of quality-teaching, investment should not be a constraint. It is yet to be known why this educational edifice crumbled mid-way and viable teacher educative programmes were phased out.

It cannot be jettisoned on the basis of poor quality of products. The country has not become all that poor, to be at the mercy of funding agencies like the World Bank.

It is reliably learnt that the World Bank sanctioned a substantial sum as loan to improve Primary Eduation in our country. Fair enough. Should it impose conditionalities such as Universalisation of Primary Education, Minimum Level of Learning, and establishment of District Institutes of Education and Training and organisation of Inservice Programmes in the Regional Colleges of Education (now renamed Regional Institutes and Education)?

Has our country totally neglected Primary Education so far and promoted only Secondary and Higher Secondary education? What is the rationale for this obsession with Primary Education? World Bank has deflected the direction of the NCERT from organising viable, regular Teacher-Education courses to the mushrooming of ill conceived Inservice Programmes in the name of promoting Minimum level of learning!

Participants in these Inservice-Programmes remain apathetic or disillusioned while the faculty members who have been coerced to conduct such programmes leaving aside regualr teaching in classes, eagerly look forward to the day of deliverance, viz. RETIREMENT/ Pretty soon we may well have to write the Epitaph of this unique Educational Experiment of the Century!

52

A Fresh Look at Refresher Courses

EDUCATION can never be looked upon as a destination point. It is always in transition. The degree or degrees obtained during graduation would wear out in a few years. It would need periodic replenishment and renewal to preserve its sheen. None would dispute this truism. Perhaps toward this purpose, several agencies such as the U.G.C. N.C.E.R.T. S.C.E.R.T. design and conduct refresher courses. Participants of such courses should not have the mind-set that they are required to undergo this training under duress. It should not be viewed as an unavoidable ordeal or some sort of respite from their routinised teaching duty. Such a blinkered vision is likely to defeat the very purpose of refresher courses.

Practitioners of a profesion such as teaching, should be imbued with a burning zeal to improve, innovate and incorporate, modified strategies of teaching transaction in class. This would enhance teacher-motivation. Teachers would do well to list down the obstacles as well as uncertainties while presenting a lesson. Whenever there is a syllabus-revision teachers raise a hue and cry because they had never had exposure to the new facts and concepts. Should they not update their content? With the rapid strides in Educational Technology the dynamics of classroom teaching have undergone a sea-change. Chalk and talk method is not altogether sidelined. But, better methods of communication have been introduced so as to activate and accelerate the learning process. Students cannot remain silent spectators or passive listeners. They become interactive participants to generate new ideas. A refresher course ought to include such inputs as are feasible in real classroom situations. Clear behavioural changes must be experienced by participants and expressed later in class. That would be the acid-test of the efficacy of the refresher course. Participants should give continuous feedback to the organising agency so that appropriate modifications are effected in future programmes.

Should a teacher be rewarded for attending a refresher course? Should it be a necessry pre-condition for promotion? Should it be voluntary or compulsory? Extrinsic benefit and inducements might rob the intrinsic benefit and plesure of participation. If only the quality of a refresher course in enhanced, interested teachers would be attracted like bees to flowers to gather honey. If it is conceived and carried out rather perfunctorily, teachers would be demotivated and disinclined.

Prof. HAYAKAWA, an authority in Linguistics delivered a series of talks at the University of Hawaii during the summer of 1961, when the author happened to be an East-West Centre Scholar. Many teachers from the mainland cities such as Los Angeles, San Francisco, Seattle and Las Vegas converged upon the campus of the University of Hawaii to register for the course and update their knowledge. Most of the participants could not be accommodated in the Lecture-hall that was literally overflowing. Live telecast of the lecture had to be arranged in several classrooms so as to help eager teachers to benefit by the series of lecturers. It refreshed them a great deal to get back to work thoroughly rejuvenated.

A lecture or a series of lectures on Welfare Economics by Prof. Amartya Sen would be the ideal tonic to motivate teachers of Economics in our Colleges and Universities. A demonstration lecture by Jayant Narlikar, would be an eye-opener to msot teachers of Astrophysics. A lecture by sharu Ranganekar or Athreya would be a shot in the arm for Management people.

Have we to ofer a bait or an incentive to attend such a course of lecturers? If a teacher chooses to remain complacent with his stock of knowledge gained during graduate days and undervalue any attempt at upgradation, he/she should be left to remain in blissful oblivion. Let him/her remain contented with the pay and perquisites of entitlement and count upon the terminal gratuity and pension. An enterprising teacher would not like to remain a cog in the wheel!

Can we assess or evaluate the benefits that accrue to the participants of a refresher course! We are yet to frame a measurement—tool. To quote Albert Einstein:

> Not everything that counts
> can be counted and not
> everything that can be counted,
> counts!

53

Another Surgery for Education

Education is a living force. It decides the destiny of a nation. Millions of citizens are its beneficiaries. Handled wrongly, it can do incalculable harm. Soon after Independence, the Government assigned top priority to improve education. Several experts examined the system and suggested remedies. They ought to have weighed judiciously the pros and cons of their recommendations. They were aware that posterity would not pardon them for their lapses.

We are yet to complete half-a-century of our Independence. Within such a short period, how often and in what haste have we brought the system to the surgical ward for surgery! Should we not be open-minded enough to do some heart-searching to realise the omissions we committed upon the recommendations of several commissions? Can we afford to ignore the collective wisdom and the precious human resources deployed in this regard? Were they so short-sighted as to provide us a plan that would be outdated so soon? We seem to have no qualms to decimate all that they prescribed. Otherwise, why should we think of preparing, another new blue-print—a 'Plan of Action'? Are we to infer that whatever was recommended by the earlier expert committees have become anachronistic and hence obsolete? Let us do a little introspection before joining the congregation of educational reformers!

Soon after Independence, the centre assigned the task of reforming University Education to a renowned scholar and diplomat. Dr. S. Radhakrishnan was not a man of mean achievement. A better person could not have been chosen. What a fine job he did in 1948! In terms of clarity, profundity and brevity, it is par excellence! Being a teacher himself, he could perceive the real danger afflicting higher education. He had the courage of conviction to be forthright because the terms of reference assigned to him was the toning up of University education. If only the Government had the Will and wisdom to implement his seminal recommenations, we would not be posing the question. "How to make a graduate employable today! Are these volumes buried in the archives of libraries?

A few years later, the Government approached Dr. A. Lakshmanaswami Mudaliar, another towering personality, to reform Secondary Edcuation in our country. He was a gynaecologist turned-academician and he adorned the chair of Vice-chancellorship of Madras University for three decades. He submitted a comprehensive report on Secondary Education in 1952 called the Mudaliar Comission Report. He could diagnose the malady afflicting School Education. He suggested diversification of Education at the Secondary stage to contain the mad rush for higher education. He recommended Multipurpose education with the result that Vocationalisation would gain respectability. But, we did not have adequate number of trained teachers to handle vocational subjects.

It was in the early Sixties that the Governemnt set up an autonomous body called the National Council of Educational Research and Training (N.C.E.R.T) to usher in a new design of Teacher education. With the Technical assistance of Ohio State University, USA, the NCERT established four Regional Colleges of Education and also a Demonstration Multipurpose School attached to each college. Four-year Integrated Programme of Teacher Education in the subjects of Commerce, Technology, Science and English were offered. We felt that the Multipurpose system of schooling advocated by Dr. A.L. Mudaliar was given a fair trial.

For reaosns best known to the decision makers, the Multipurpose school system was given up. Demonstration Multipurpose schools dropped the middle name and the Regional colleges of Educaton closed unceremoniously the Commerce and Technology streams in Teacher-education. It resulted in the wastage of infrastructure and underutilisation of Human Resources. After having axed the vocational courses that were designed to prepare teachers for the Multipurpose Schools the decison-makers are now pleading for vocationalisation! Here is another instance of wasted human resources!

In the early Sixties, the Govenment requested an eminent Professor of Physics in Delhi University to prepare a Comprehensive Report covering all stages of education. Dr. D.S. Kothari enlistd the services of several educationists in the country and prepared a detailed Report in 1964. It was called Education Commission Report or Kothari Commission Report. It can be considered the watershed in the realm of education in the post-independence era! He pleaded for vocationalisation and recommended a meaningful activity covering Primary as well as High School Stages known as Socially Useful Productive Work (SUPW). He also underscored the need for a Guidance and Counselling centre in Secondary Schools so as to minimise the incidence of vocational misfits. It is a matter of regret that even in the Demonstration Schools attached to the Regional Colleges of Edcuation, the Guidance Counsellor's post remained permanently vacant. If only the recommendation of Dr. Kothari were sincerely implemented, we may not need a revision of education policy at least till the turn of the century. No one has come out with a convincing argument as to why the valuable recommendations of the Education Commission were sidelined!

In any other country, these stalwarts—Dr. S. Radhakrishnan, Dr. A.L. Mudaliar and Dr. D.S. Kothari — would have been honoured and hailed as the pace setters of educational reconstruction. Have we bothered to calculate the time, labour and the utilisation of precious human resources involved in these exercises in futility?

Rajiv Gandhi was instrumental to the next shake-up in education. He activated the NCERT to prepare a New Educational Policy and a Programme of Action (N.E.P. and P.O.A.) to inject fresh blood and also to introduce innovative projects. It can hardly match the elegance and profundity of earlier Reports. It is nothing but a rehash of the Education Commision Report (1964) with a sprinkling of a few fancy schemes. Operation Blackboard Scheme kept everyone guessing! No one could explain how such a term was coined! It occupied the centre state in all seminars and workshops. It is slowly recedng to the background. The buzz words now are DIET (District Institutes of Education and Training) and MLL (Minimum Levels of Learning).

In spite of all these jargons schools are fast becoming coaching shops with rampant commecialisation. Teacher pupil contact in now replaced by teacher-pupil contract. The Universities are losing their sheen by promoting unbriddled proliferation of Correspndence courses. The examination wing of the University has become a hotbed of corruption and manipulation. Professional courses like Medicine and Engineering have become lucrative business centres for the unscrupulous promoters. There is no dearth of funds. The budget allocation for education keeps expanding. We only need to remind ourselves of the prophetic pronouncement of Dr. Kothari in his Education Commission Report: "DESTINY OF A NATION IS BEING SHAPED IN THE CLASSROOM."

54

What it Takes to be a Good Teacher

A PROFESSION is different form a trade. Members of a profession voluntarily impose upon themselves certain rules and regulations. To a considerable extent they themselves perform the dual function of execution and inspection.

Apart from the statutory provisions enjoined on the supervisory personnel, every teacher functions within the constraints of his own conscience. It has to be intrinsically goaded. It was this aspect that earned the teaching profession the prefix "noble" in bygone days. Posterity would certainly blame us if we do not re-establish the pre-eminence the teacher enjoyed once upon a time and refurbish the lost image of the profession. It is appropriate to abide by certain restraints or commandments.

1. Never enter the profession of teaching unless you have an instinctive urge to mingle with growing minds. You don't necessarily have to undergo any sophisticated screening procedure to fulfil this condition. All you need to do is to visit a few classrooms, spend some time, watch and also communicate with a few kids, as well as their teachers, to understand the dynamics of classroom teaching. It is advisable to visit quite a variety of schools so that you do not commit

the error of biased sampling. Sit down and calmly think whether you will not regret your choice.

2. Never step into teach unless you are convinced you have infinite patience.

Teaching is not always rewarding in the sense you would achieve what you aimed at. It is human to hanker after positive results; but beyond human nature to accept failure. You might fail to do your job satisfactorily despi:e your sincere efforts. Be patient. You will improve, provided you desire to improve.

What about your students' indifference? Would you pull them up or push them out or pat them? Remember, you are charged with the responsibility of sowing the seed of learning, nurturing and developing it so that the students could later on function independently and autonomously. Intemperate handling of innocent kids is blasphemy, if not infanticide!

3. Never aspire to multiply your material possession pursuing the profession of teaching.

Very few realise the truth that one has to sacrifice more than amassing wealth. It calls for an attitude of self-abnegation.

A teacher has to enlarge his heart rather than his estate. Every child has to have a place in the teacher's heart. If you barter your knowledge for a few more rupees, you become a trader and a mercenary. If you have no confidence in your integrity, never become a teacher.

4. Practise before your preach.

A teacher wields considerable sway over his students. He is older, mature and also balanced to advise his studnets. Unfortunately, this prerogative in likely to be misused. He tends to preach more than he can practise.

"Speak the truth;" "Honesty is the best policy;" "Perservance pays'" "Procrastination in the thief of time;" "An idle mind in the devil's worship;" "A friend in need is a friend indeed;" "Rome is not built in a day.....

None would dispute the veracity of these maxims. These morals have to be functional rather than pontifical; down-to-earth rather thn ethereal. An honest teacher who is not afraid of speaking the truth at all times earns respect from his students:

5. Be creative and innovative.

A non-creative teacher tends to get bored after a few years of teaching. The rest of his career would be repetitive and restive. One has to plan one's lesson, but one cannot plan in advance how one would teach it. It can take a myriad forms, depending upon his mood, réceptivity of the students and the resources available. A teacher needs to replenish his knowledge constantly, discard the obsolete and be innovative in his/her approach. This is the only antidote to monotony and stereotyping. Such a teacher tends to be exuberant till the day of his retirement.

6.b Do not hanker after popularity.

Students often brand a teacher as a disciplinarian, an inveterate bore or a hard task-master. Certainly these are not complimentary epithets. Many a student in your class would have cursed you for engaging the class till the last minute or even a little beyond. They might have even mildly hissed to register their silent protest over your prolonged lecture. A section of them would certainly have blamed you for the harsh criticism you had relentlessly made on their sub-standard assignment. You might have made them sweat, labour and suffer like anything. But, in their heart of hearts, they might be unwittingly worshipping you for eliciting the best form them. Remember, a teacher is not a mass entertainer.

He does not have to be humorous, though a witty anecdote in an appropriate context would be a welcome digression. If you begin to yield beyond the respectable limit to the immature demands of your students, you would become unpopular.

7. Set realistic goals and strive hard to attain these.

Life without a goal is like navigating on a rudderless ship. Every student in your class in endowed with certain potentialities. Given the appropriate environmental stimulation, each one is bound to blossom. Your job is to assess the merits of each student and also be aware of his limits. Societal demands, parental pressures and peer-group competition tend to obfuscate the perspective of the students and prompt them to pursue an unrealistic goal. Your responsibility is to set right their vision and help them reach attainable goals.

8. Never underestimate your students.

Experienced teachers have a temptation to develop an exaggerated image of themselves and look down upon their wards as if they are fledglings. Students are young, immature and inexperienced, no doubt. But, some among them could be really intelligent and even outsmart you by their incisive questioning. Remain a humble teacher.

9. Be proud to be a teacher.

Materialistic values have taken such deep roots in society that the worth of an individual in correlated with the money he makes. While you cannot make money in teaching, you can certainly make minds. Do not surrender your self-regard to those who profess materialistic values. You may not save much. But you will not starve. Teachers, since time immemorial, have belonged to a privileged class. Their life transcends the lives of those they serve and the lighter they are with regard to their material possessions, the higher they ascend in their aims and aspirations.

55

Let us Learn to Respect Our Teachers

SEPTEMBER 5th is a red-letter day for us. All over the country functions are held to honour our teachers. The philosopher—President, the late Dr. Radhakrishnan was born on that day. He started his career as a teacher and made a mark in that profession. His erudition and eloquence won him world-recognition Wherever he went he spread the gospel of Indian Philosophy with courage and conviction. Posterity would remember him not merely as a President but as a great teacher and philosopher. It behoves us to bear in mind the yeoman services rendered by teachers on the birthday of a great teacher.

In our sriptures it is said:

> "Respect you mother; respect your father, and respect your teacher." Mother is the first person with whom an infant comes into contact. She protects and brings up her child during the formative period. Later father shares the responsibility.

Every child identifies itself with the father. When the parents hand over the child to the care of a teacher in a school, the teacher becomes a parent-substitute. All the honour and affection a child bestows upon parents would be transferred to the perceptor. A child has to love the teacher first and then only respect, because love is the foundation on which respect is built.

When sage Viswamitra wanted to take Rama along with him to the forest, king Dasaratha was reluctant and was about to refuse. But, he was prevailed upon by Sage Vasishta not to do so. Rama learnt many things form the sage in the forest that he would never have learnt in Ayodhya. Viswamitra might have been a terror to his contemporaries, but to Rama he was a great teacher and a kind counsellor.

A child admitted into a nursery school gets panicky and cries when the mother is away. The gentle hug of a kind teacher and her soft-spoken words soon transform her into a mother in the mind of the child. The child sits on the lap of her teacher as she would do with her mother. Yet, when her own mother turns up in the evening the child runs away form the teacher to join her mother. By and by, the teacher establishes her hold on the child and gradually weans her away form home. She teaches many things that could not be learnt form parents. All the time the teacher realises that she could win the child's confidence, only by love and not by threat on command. A child's love toward her teacher later gets transferred to the subject she teaches. If a child were to dread and hate a teacher then the hatred gets transferred to the subject she teaches.

Few of us realise how much we owe our teachers who spent countless hours teaching us the alphabet, numerals and stories of valour and heroism. "Whether we shine as a salesman, a lawyer, an inspector of Police, a judge—why, even as a teacher, it is due to the blessings of our teachers.

It is really sad to note that the teacher who helped so many of us to climb up the ladder of life has himself to live in misery and want. What we pay him is not commensurate with his contribution to society. Why, he is not even given an appropriate status in society. When will our people learn to respect the teaching community? Perhaps, the various ills that afflict humanity at large could be attributed to this apathy and ingratitude. Let us learn to honour our teachers.

"The man who would be truly happy should not study to enlarge his estates, but to contract his desires".

—Plato.

"The secret of happiness is to learn to accept the impossible, do without the indispensable and bear the intolerable".

—Bishop Mandell Creighton.

56

A Golden Past, and Future

I am not one of those chronic pessimists to despair and dwell on the downward trend in Education. It is not fair to overlook the lush greenery and stare at the shrubs and stones.

At every stage in evolution people did reflect nostalgically on the good old golden days. To the extent that this invigorates and kindles hope for a better tomorrow it is energising and exciting. Once it compels an individual to get back to the pleasant past and renounce the present, it ceases to be a pragmatic programme of action.

Students in modern schools are certainly active, exuberant and goal-directed. Right from infancy they get conditioned to a regimen and strictly adhere to a schedule. They are trained to wake-up early, eat quickly and get ready smartly, to be on time at school. Whether they walk or cycle or carried by a van is of little consideration. What is noteworthy is the healthy habit of overcoming lethargy and indolence. Such characteristics would be desirable not only during the formative years, but also in future.

In terms of the theory of relativity, one seldom finds time hanging heavily when it is packed with purposeful activity. The spate of advertisements in the electronic media highlights this, whether it is using a brand of toothpaste or a toilet soap or a beverage!

Sometimes parents point out these to boys and girls and urge the children to emulate them. The presentation of celebrities like Sachin Tendulkar or Viswanathan Anand lends credence as well, though grown-ups would be wiser to sift fact from fancy.

Fortunately, every school has some teachers who serve as role-models. Their dress, manners, speech, devotion to duty, concern for pupil-progress and welfare, do impress the youth a great deal. Among the teaching community one could find a few actualised individuals too-those who explicitly reveal the thrill and ecstasy of deep study, reflection and relaxation.

Perhaps such teachers might not be 'coaching' students for a competitive examination or computer wizardry. They might get lost while reading out Wordsworth's "Solitary Reaper" or William Blake', "Tyger Tyger". Or, they might dwell at length on how Carl Gauss discovered the Theory of Probability or how Archimedes ran across the streets of Syracuse shouting 'Eureka' 'Eureka'.

In a limited sense such teachers actualise their potentialities. If only a few among the students were to imbibe and emulate such teachers to become teachers, we would be ushering in a golden future similar to the golden past!

57

The Head that Wears the Crown!

The burning desire of most persons who step into the profession of Teaching is to ascend somehow the top position in a school, presumably to enjoy the pseudo-privilege of being a Principal or Headmaster. Pretty soon they would realise that it was after all a mirage, certainly not worth bartering the pride and pleasure they commanded in a classroom wherein inquisitive learners were eager to sponge every word uttered by dedicated teachers.

No doubt the Principal's chamber might look posh, well furnished, with one or more telephones plus a computer that would keep on flashing and flickering the goings-on around the campus. Cups and rolling shields won by students in Inter-school competitions might adorn the cup-boards, adding aura to the room. Encyclopaedia volumes and some of the famous classics of renowned authors too would be showcased. Where is the time for the Principal to browse through, let alone read leisurely those classics!

The gentleman seated on the throne seldom enjoys the peace and tranquillity that he experienced in abundance as a newly appointed teacher. Sooner or later one might forget the subject one taught with passion and devotion because of the pinpricks associated with administration. Those colleagues who were so close and intimate in the past tend to maintain a distance. Quite a few disgruntled seniors might even hatch a plot surreptitiously to malign and bring down the image of the Head. No wonder such Heads return home everyday with headaches. Some seek solace from stress-management programmes that have mushroomed all over the country!

Let us pose ourselves a few questions. Why does a person choose the profession of teaching? To be away from the madding crowd so as to enjoy the agony and ecstasy of teaching on this good earth, a teacher finds peace in a classroom. The thrill in sharing the knowledge and wisdom one gained with those who wish to gain, cannot be described adequately. The excitement experienced by a teacher after delivering a lesson on "Electricity and Magnetism" or "Mendel's Laws of Heredity" or "The History of the Freedom struggle" or the elegance of "Elegy, written in a country churchyard", cannot be estimated in monetary terms.

When a teacher enjoys teaching, students enjoy learning. When a teacher endures teaching, students endure learning. What is enjoyed endures. What is endured does not endure! Such a teacher returns home everyday with a feeling of supreme satisfaction. He might plan for a better delivery of the same topic to a different section the following day. The more a teacher gives, the more he gains. With limited needs and easier fulfilment, he is neither greedy nor needy. He chooses to remain a ladder upon which his students could climb and scale new heights, far beyond the reach of their preceptors. Does not everyone need a ladder to ascend in life?

In contrast, the Head of an institution would return home pretty exhausted, with a feeling of exasperation on account of the commissions and omissions of the teaching and non-teaching staff. He has to keep a tab on every single aspect of teaching and administration because their blunders would boomerang unpredictably. Some parents might barge into his chamber to report about the ineptitude of some teachers. These days the head of an Institution is compelled to do tight-rope walking as he cannot pull up any of his subordinates for their dereliction of duty. Because it might trigger a kind of revolt and precipitate a crisis - strike!

Sooner or later, the head of an Institution would realise he has lost his head and that the chair he was so anxious to occupy was only a thorny one! He would reminisce over the pleasant decades of the past as a humble classroom teacher and the rewards he received therefrom. Countless teachers retire as teachers and they are remembered by countless students for their exemplary teaching. They count on their teachers for all they gained in life!

When Dr. A.P.J. Abdul Kalam, Principal Scientific Advisor to Government of India was interviewed by Doordarshan soon after he was conferred the coveted honour of Bharat Ratna, he only recollected his humble teacher, Sri. Sivasubramania Iyer, who taught him in the elementary school at Rameswaram in his third standard. This teacher instilled in the young boy of seven the quest for scientific temper that catapulted him to the pinnacle as a great scientist!

To quote Ralph Waldo Emerson:

"Not gold, but only teachers can make
A people great and strong-
Men who for truth and honour's, sake
Stand fast and suffer long
It is they who build a nation's pillar deep
And lift them to the sky."

58

A Teacher's Reminiscences

These days most teachers, at all levels, have, grievances for redressal than nostalgic remembrances of the golden periods of their career. What an irony! Very few professions, barring the medical profession, leaves lasting impressions on one's psyche than the profession of teaching. It is immaterial at what level-Primary or secondary or beyond - one is called upon to render this service. Service with a smile is what is expected of those who choose to be teachers. It is not meant for all and sundry, but only a select few who give more than receive in return.

Every year one meets new young faces in the class, expectant, eager, enquiring minds, listening attentively to someone whom they would like to adore and emulate. I recollect a humble, simple but great teacher who influenced me a great deal in my sixth standard. He was short-statured but was not short of zest and zeal to mould us. He was a scout-master too: Shifting his head upward and downward, with a protruding nose, he would train us in the proper pronunciation of words such as One, Honest and Opportunity. Though more than half-a-century has elapsed, such delectable memories remain ever green in my mind. I do not know whether he was adequately compensated by the school he served. But, he was always clad in spotless white khadi dhoti and jibba, with his forehead proclaiming his Vaishnavite faith!

I could even recollect his stentorian voice and the uninhibited laughter he would burst into quite often. I never thought I would join the very profession that he pursued with aplomb. To him teaching was a mission, to be carried on with passion and devotion than a trade to be transacted for a price!

I had a drill-master at school in the mid-forties (before Independence). He was also in his mid-forties! But, he would look like someone in his early thirties! He would ask us, all boys, to line up in the sprawling ground and blow his whistle at intervals to which we stretched our legs and arms forward, upward and side ward and come back to position. To my young mind, it never occurred to me why he insisted on everyone performing these exercises unerringly.

A friend of mine, a clumsy lad, would be giggling and committing silly mistakes. The drill-master would catch hold of him and beat nicely with the twig of a tree and make him behave. It would be a reign of terror. Now, when I see Tendulkar, Dravid and Ganguly obeying the coach and performing funny exercises before participating in a triangular Cricket tournament, I recollect my school days and the far-sighted drill-master! He groomed me to be a Volleyball player. By the time I reached eleventh standard I grew taller than my teacher. He was more a friend than a teacher to me. Though I do not have his photograph with me, his face is permanently etched in my mind.

With little awareness of what is meant by Psychology, I opted for this subject in my Intermediate class. I was captivated by the teacher, young and handsome, clad in silk jibba and dhoti with a cherubic face, brightened by his fair complexion and well-combed hair. He would enter the class with irrepressible enthusiam. An elementary textbook for beginners by an author was prescribed. My teacher would, however, refer advanced books for teaching. We would listen to him with rapt attention. Every word uttered by him would be precise. Now and then he would dictate a definition and follow it up by explanation. Only then, did I make up my mind to be a teacher like him.

Having retired from the teaching profession some ten years ago, I recall with nostalgia the days I stuttered and stammered during the initial stage of my career, how I cried in privacy over my ineptitude, how I received encouragement from my Principal and senior colleagues and how I learnt to enjoy teaching, promoted discussion among students and endeavoured my best to make them good human beings! If only every teacher were to strive hard to give of his best in class and stir the imagination of students, what a glorious innings would they have had in life!

"We hate some people because we don't know them;
we will not know them because we hate them.

—*Charles C. Colton.*

59

The Talented Turbaned Teachers

Present-day children wear uniform dress to school. No uniform is prescribed for teachers. But, the accepted attire of teacher of bygone days was pure white khadi jibba or close coat with 'Pancha Cucha', Angavastram and a turban. It was easy to distinguish the teacher from other people in the community. Regardless of the salary they earned, their very appearance exuded majesty and earned regard from everyone. They were quite parsimonious in their smile and perhaps some never smiled at all! Students would do all within their powers to please them and earn from them at least a few compliments. Even while praising a student they would observe economy and simply say, "keep it up."

Later, pant and coat replaced dhoti and angavastra, but turban continued to be used by some teachers. None would have ever seen the renowned Vice-chancellor of Madras University, Dr. A Lakshmanaswamy Mudaliar, one who strode like a Colossus for well over a quarter century, without his turban and the "Namam" upon his forehead. He would look serene and serious all the time. No politician had ever ventured to go anywhere near him. He was an eminent surgeon as well as an academician. His valued friend Prof. Krishnamoorthy, Principal of Pachaiappa's College, a commandingly tall figure, with a stentorian voice would don a long coat, "Pancha Cucha" and a turban. Students used to look forward to his lecture and his very presence would quieten everyone in the class or corridor.

Dr. Sarvapalle S. Radhakrishnan mesmerised his students by his lectures on Western and Eastern Philosophy during his days in Mysore University. With his long coat, rimless glasses, radiant smile and turban, he commanded respect from his colleagues as well as students. It was his scholarship that earned him the position of President of India. Pandit Nehru was happy that the illustrious Professor condescended to accept the position of President of India. His turban added elegance to his personality.

Equally eminent persons like Sir. C.P. Ramaswami Iyer, Right Honouable Srinivasa Sastri, Sir. C.V. Raman, Sri. Stayamoorthy- all wore turbans. An outstanding Headmaster of Besant Theosophical school, Madras, Sri. Balakrishna Joshi would always wear a cap and his eloquence would be the envy of teachers of his days. We cannot say that there is a positive correlation between wearing turban and achieving eminence. But, quite a few instances like the renowned lawyers like Alladi Krishnaswami Iyer, A.S. Panchapakesa Iyer, Annamalai Cheltiar (Foudner of Annamalai University) seem to warrant some correlation between one's dress and eminence.

One might ask, "What is in a dress?" There is everything in it. It adds to the prestige of the profession one occupies and it constantly urges him to uphold the dignity. A turbaned person will never be crest fallen, because the turban would fall down. He would always hold his head high and erect. It reminds him of his duty to be dedicated, disciplined and service-minded! It would distinguish him from the rest in clear terms.

Present day teachers dress quite casually. Has it made them casual in teaching too? It seems so. Students find it difficult to respect such teachers. They socialise too much. Of course, one should not go by mere outward appearnace, but go deeper into the worth of a person. The instances of poor teaching or lack of accountability were considerably less among the traditional, turbaned teachers. One who wears a turban does not spend much time in combing and grooming the hair. Apparent smartness is not real smaıtness. If only half the time in combing hair is spent on reviewing and rehearsing what one should teach, most teachers would experience the thrill of teaching like the old-timers!

> "If a man will begin with certainties, he shall end in doubt; but if he will be content to begin with doubt, he shall end in certainties."
>
> — *Francis Bacon.*

60

Those Good Old Days!...

Fifty years in the history of a nation is not a short period. It is long enough to establish worthy models and traditions.

During the early days of emancipation from the British rule we never stopped criticising and condemning the system of education that promoted the production of clerks and officials to assist the royals of the British in ruling Indians. We sent away those fair-skinned foreigners, lock, stock and barrel, and installed in their position our own experts in Education. Perhaps those pilgrim-fathers realised the trust reposed on them and rendered self-less service. We had Dr. S. Radhakrishnan, Dr. A.L. Mudaliar, Dr. Kothari who headed separate commissions so as to make education a vital force for national reconstruction.

Alas! Those volumes are gathering dust in the archives of our libraries. It has become unfashionable to even quote these Reports in modern educational seminars and conferences. Informed people sneer and scorn at the very mention of these Reports as though these are the artefacts of bygone days. Have these Reports lost their relevance for improving educational standards!

While I do not condemn some of the ultra-modern jargons such as "Education for all"; "Minimum levels of learning"; "National Education Policy; "Teacher Empowerment"; "School

Effectiveness" and related mumbo jumbo, what disturbs me most is the impatience with which we usher in and also withdraw reforms in education.

In the forties and fifties too, we had Primary schools and the teachers therein rendered no mean service to humanity. They knew what they had to do and their accountability was unassailable, and their integrity above reproach. There was personalised attention in class and pupils seldom reacted wildly when they received punishment for their misdemeanors. The bond between the teacher and the taught never got snapped though the recalcitrant ones were subdued by the authority of preceptors. Some students performed under duress but did they hate their teachers on this account?

Teachers had greater faith upon their communicative ability than on improvised teaching aids. They had not even heard of overhead projectors or computers! Shorn of fancy furniture or uniforms and shoes and high-tech gymnasium, children squatted and listened to teachers with rapt attention and exercised their memory far more than the modern kids. The cost of good education for Std I today was adequate to meet the cost of school as well as collegiate education of yester-year. Every teacher respected the headmaster and never indulged in character assassination or any such calumny. Vigorous games in the evening were invariably found in all school play-grounds. Those who graduated from this old-fashioned education did occupy coveted positions in society. Never did we come across a single instance of malpractice.

Private tuition did prevail even in those days. Not always for fees! Some taught children during week-ends and never collected any fees for this extra service. Rather they felt happy that some children were genuinely interested in clarifying their doubts.

All through primary classes children used only slates. In high-school they were provided black-lead pencils and erasers. Only upon entry into college could they request for fountainpens. Ball-point pens never existed. No one heard the word "Donation" and parents never had to spend nightmarish days to educate children. Classrooms were less crowded and assessment fair. Detention was accepted as permissible deterrent for slackness and slovenliness.

Have I conducted the readers on an Utopian tour of unbelievable transparency and simplicity? It is time we woke up to reality and mobilised money for admission to the kindergarten in an English medium school! Let us keep up with Joneses and join the ranks of overburdened parents to provide quality - education to their progeny!

> "In nature there are neither rewards nor punishments- there are consequences".
>
> —*Robert G. Ingersoll.*

> "There is no duty we so much underrate as the duty of being happy"
>
> —*Robert Louis Stevenson.*

61

Imaginative Teaching

Teaching is not just talking or speaking to a class of students. It is much more serious and goal-directed. Within a time frame one has to accomplish as much as possible. The recipients must leave the class with a feeling of fulfilment. There is no place for undue embellishment or uncalled for digression. One has to be conscius all the time whether a lesson is progressing or stagnant.

A plan is a kind of blueprint that incorporates all the relevant inputs that should go into a lesson. It should also include periodic feedback from students that constitutes what is called FORMATIVE EVALUATION. We normally think that testing in done toward the end of a lesson. Of course we do test student's understanding of a lesson toward the completion of a unit. That is called SUMMATIVE EVALUATION.

In the absence of a planned instruction, teaching is reduced to a kind of haphazard presentation. Often a teacher might feel at the end of a class that he had spent too much time on trivialities and too little time on significant aspects. A good deal of preparation is called for on the part of a teacher regardless of his/her experience in teaching.

In Teachers Training college, a trainee is taught the nuances of planning a lesson and even trained to perfect each skill in a micro-situation. One cannot afford to be deficient in blackboard work, use of teaching aids, questioning technique, encouragement of pupil-participation etc., etc. Several components constitute the amalgam of successful teaching. A novice in the profession is trained to perfect each skill and try-out these in an integrated manner in actual classroom. Let us dwell at length upon each aspect.

A teacher has to state in clear behavioural terms the over-all objective of teaching a lesson. It is always in a global from such as: "To enable the students to understand and appreciate the emergence of truth as a result of experimentation than fond belief or superstition—Science. All lessons in Science will have such a pervading objective. However, this needs delineation into specific, explicit behaviours that can be observed and evaluated. Here is an illustration:

SALTS DISSOLVE in water. Take a spoon of common salt—SODIUM CHLORIDE—and add it to the water in a beaker. Stir gently. The CRYSTALS settle down at the bottom and disappear after a few minutes. Add one more spoon of salt and stir. It also disappears.. Water becomes less TRANSPARENT when salt is dissolved. Keep on adding salt till such time you find a SEDIMENT of salt that does not get dissolved. This is called a SATURATED SOLUTION. If the solution is heated, salt would get dissolved sooner. Beyond a certain level salt cannot be dissolved even by heating. Continued heating would cause EVAPORATION of water and CRYSTALLISATION of salt.

The bold lettered terms are called CONCEPTS, because these can be generalised. Students observe simple demonstration of experiment and infer. There is no place for assumption here. They can repeat the same experiment anywhere and obtain similar results. As a result of this simple experiment a teacher does justice to the global or general objective as well as the specific objective of elucidating the concept of SATURATION.

Experimentation is not the monopoly of scientists alone. It is found in every discipline. It varies in substance and form. We know that language is a vehicle of thought. It has to adhere to a common code of rules—Grammar. How does a child pick up several sounds of a language? How does the vocal chord function? Do other parts of the human anatomy like nose, tongue, teeth, lungs, windpipe also function in unison to enable us to perfect speech? Let us examine:

> The first cry by a child is the cry of birth. Early sounds are explosive in nature—caused by the air being expelled from the lungs through the vocal chords. Learning a language is due to the interaction of maturation and learning. A certain amount of neurophysiological growth is necessary. The normal acquisition of speech sounds is mediated by a process of PHONEME EXPANSION which is controlled by maturation and a process of PHONEME CONTRACTION which is influenced by social interactions with individuals in a particular language-culture. PHONEME means a unit of sound which makes a difference in the meaning of words. It refers to 'vowel' and 'Consonant´ sounds of a language. 'Vowel' is a speech sound in which air passes in a continuous stream through the open mouth. e.g. a, e, i, o, u.
>
> 'Consonant' is a letter representing a speech-sound made by obstructing the breath stream e.g. p, t, l. 'Diphthong' is a sound made by gliding from one vowel to another in one syllable, e.g. as in 'oil.' 'Nasal'is uttered with breath passing through the nose.'Speech' involves the use of the lungs, the

wind pipe the voice box, the throat, the palate, the nose, the tongue, the lips and the teeth.

The above mentioned terms constitute the components of language learning. A teacher has to be fully aware of these aspects to promote learing among students. Let us examine how the structure of language is taught at the high-school level.

Sentences have two kinds of STRUCTURES SURFACE structure and DEEP structure. Examine this sentence:

"Harry is willing to help".

'Harry' is a noun; "is" a verb; 'willing' an adjective; 'to' a preposition; and 'help' a verb the last two combined in an infinitive (surface structure).

The term "Deep structure" refers to the relationship of the concepts being represented by the words in the 'surface structure'. Read the following sentence:

'Harry is difficult to help.'

In terms of 'surface grammar' the two sentences are alike. The only difference between them is the words 'willing' in one sentence and the word "difficult" in the other. Both are adjectives and both are in the same position in the sentence. On further analysis, however, there are important differences between the sentences.

In 'Harry is difficult to help", 'Harry' is the person to be helped. Technically, in the first sentence "Harry" is the subject of the verb 'help'. In the second, he is the object.

Whatever we teach must evoke a sense of awe and wonder. Students should be thrilled and excited. An imaginative teacher can accomplish this. WILLIAM JAMES observes:

> "If a teacher were to explain the distance of the Sun from the Earth, let him ask.... If any one there in the Sun fired off a cannon straight at you, what should you do?

"Get out of the way" would be the answer.

> "No need of that" the teacher might reply "you may quietly go to sleep in your room and get up again. You may wait until your graduation day. You may learn a trade and grow old as I am — then only the cannon ball will be getting near; then you may jump to one side. See, so great as that is the sun's distance.

Prof. JAYANT NARLIKAR, the renowned Astrophysicist cited an interesting ancedote while delivering a lecture at the National Science Exhibition for children in 1976 in New Delhi. He quoted the famous British Astronomer, EDDINGTON:

> "He compared man's position in the universe with that of a potato-bug in a potato inside a sack placed in the basement of a ship, floating on the sea, trying to know what the sea is like. So in the same way, we are in this planet of a solar system which is part of a galaxy and which is, in turn, a part of the system of galaxies in a small part of the universe and we are trying to look through all these limitations what is beyond."

To sum up, a teacher has to possess fertile imagination to make the lessons absorbing. His interest in the subject should not dry up. When a teacher enjoys teaching, students enjoy learning. When a teacher endures teaching students too endure learning. What is enjoyed endures. What is endured does not endure!

62

Debating Pedagogy

Pedagogy is the science and art of teaching. Learning and teaching function in tandem. Every one engaged in the task of teaching would be benefitted by appropriate pedagogical training. Regardless of the level at which one functions—pre-primary, primary, secondary, higher secondary, collegiate and University—some amount of training would undoubtedly increase one's teaching competency. While we have a training course for teachers at lower levels, we waive this requirement to the functionaries at the collegiate and University levels. Is it not necessary to break this convention and introduce a statutory regulation of appropriate pedagogical training for teachers at the upper levels? We use high sounding designations such as Professors, Readers, and Lecturers for college/university level teaching. The humble lot at school-level are called Trained graduate Teachers and Post-graduate Teachers. The compensation package is proportionately scaled down.

Should we underestimate the role of those who lay the foundation to make schooling enjoyable and sustainable? Should we also exaggerate the role of the elite at the upper strata? Montessori, professionally a medical doctor, elevated primary level teaching by designing an appropriate strategy of training. It does require qualified, committed teachers to teach little children. Sensation leads to perception and perception determines conceptualisation.

The first two cognitive exercises pave the way for higher cognitive processes. By and large college and university level teachers deal with concepts which involve a great deal of abstraction and generalisation. Nevertheless the keel of the ship should not be leaky. Needs of learners vary according to age. Children at the primary level need freedom to play, explore, manipulate and hence education must be predominantly activity-based. High-school teachers need training to handle preadolescent learners. Classroom dynamics differ.

At the higher-secondary level, teachers have to deal with adolescent students who tend to be a little more boisterous, if not belligerent. They are prone to a kind of negativism and pseudo-maturity. They face identity-crisis. This is also the juncture when students begin their journey towards professional courses.

Naturally, there would be a need for teacher-counsellors to handle them. Even at the college/University level, they would need appropriate guidance to develop self-esteem and self-determination. To say that no kind of pedagogical training is necessary for teachers at the higher levels reflects short sightedness.

Teaching-Learning Symbiosis

Barring notable exceptions most teachers at the collegiate and University levels just deliver lectures to a large or small class without expecting any kind of feedback from the learners. In striking contrast to the lively interaction at school level, learners at the higher level tend to remain relatively passive. One may even notice a sense of complacency among teachers while structuring and delivering lecturers.

It is assumed that a sound knowledge of the subject would suffice to survive in class. Only when they conduct tests or examinations do they realise how hollow the comprehension of most students is. Unlike school teachers who would feel guilty upon the mediocre performance of students in tests, college teachers, by and large, tend to remain detached and nonchalant. They would expect the students to be more accountable and responsible. Do their expectations prove true?

Teachers give a long list of readings for reference work. Do they monitor and check how many of the students really carried out their instructions? Do they have time and concern to visit the library to observe whether their students put in the required hours of reading and note taking? The kind of permissiveness noticed among students may not be conducive to disciplined learning. Even today, students at school hold their teachers in high esteem and do make an effort to obey their instructions. Teachers too reciprocate this trust.

The absence of such a teacher-student symbiosis at the higher level could be the main cause of underachievement at graduate and post graduate levels. What kind of training could we conceive of for college teachers?

Expository Teaching

Lecturing and teaching are not synonymous. We can learn a lot from psychologist David Ausubel, who argued for Expository Teaching methodology, which paves way for meaningful Reception learning. He was not disputing the utility of Discovery Learning recommended by Jerome S. Bruner. Bruner, who had his grounding in the theory of Cognitive Development developed by Piaget, the Swiss psychologist, swore by Discovery Learning. Undoubtedly personal first-hand, direct experience always remains superior to listening to verbal instruction in class. We learn gardening not by reading books, but by actually soiling our hands and fingers. Does it mean that every bit of knowledge gained is always the result of first-hand experience? Is there no need for verbal instruction in class? Should we not lay the foundation of listening comprehension among pupils by which we not only enlarge their vocabulary but also make learning meaningful? Do students passively listen to a lecture or actively assimilate what the teacher is expounding?

As students ascend to higher levels of learning/education they realise they have a lot of subjects to study within a shorter period of time. Teachers have the responsibility of conveying large amount of information meaningfully within a time-frame. They need to prefect their skill in lucid presentation. David Ausubel calls this Expository method resulting in Meaningful Reception Learning.

Ausubel contrasts Reception Learning with Rote Learning or Blind memorisation. Whatever is learnt by students without adequate comprehension is not assimilated. It is soon forgotten. Reception Learning is an organisation of the events of instruction that relies primarily on the teacher or on resource-materials to instruct the learner—to direct his attention, form relationships for him, and even tell him answers—at each step of the learning sequence. It follows deductive method. There is nothing inherent in a Reception approach, nor for that matter in a discovery approach that guarantees meaningful learning. Meaningful Learning or Rote learning can result from either approach as shown below:

	Discovery	*Reception*
Meaningful	Meaningful Discovery	Meaningful Reception
Rote	Rote Discovery	Rote Reception

Ausubel believes that pupils learn by organising new information, placing it into coding systems. Ausubel calls the general concept at the top of the coding system the Subsumer, because all other concepts are subsumed under it. He believes that learning should progress deductively, that is from an understanding of the general concepts to an understanding of specifics. Concepts, principles and ideas are presented to them. The more organised and meaningful the presentation the more thoroughly the person will learn.

Simply memorising the content of the Text or Lecture is not meaningful. Connections must be made with the student's existing knowledge. Rote memorisation is a very ineffective learning strategy. Expository teaching calls for a great deal of interaction between the teacher and the students. It makes greater use of examples. It is deductive. It is sequential.

Cognitive Structure and Structure of Discipline

An individual is likely to form on the basis of experiences a structure of thought, namely cognitive structure. This structure originates as a simple one like, "A ball thrown above falls on the ground;" "A spoon of salt added to water gets dissolved;" Ice-cream exposed to atmospheric temperature gets melted in a few minutes." Every such observation builds in a student some fundamental concepts.

As one studies various subjects one notices individual structure for Physics, Botany, Chemistry and so on. When an individual's cognitive structure "interacts" with the "structures" of various disciplines, a "matching process" starts. There is a hierarchy of organisation in every discipline whereby broad and abstract concepts are placed lower, depending upon the levels of complexity. A sort of "Pyramidal structure" is formed. Every time a teacher introduces a new concept an "Information Processing" exercise arises. An "intellectual Mapping" takes place. When there is a "Potential

Fit" between the existing cognitive structure and the new structure of a discipline, "understanding" takes place, resulting in expansion and enrichment of the thinking process. Therefore, while presenting information verbally, a teacher has to employ words so skilfully that the learner will not encounter any difficulty in "hooking" the new knowledge with the existing cognitive structure. The new knowledge does not remain new any more because it merges with the existing structure. Whatever is verbally presented gets converted into meaningful knowledge when the learner processes the information. Expository Teaching emphasises this part of communication. It is by experience a teacher learns the art of conveying information in a lucid style. An illustration of cognitive structure is given below:

An Illustration of Cognitive Structure

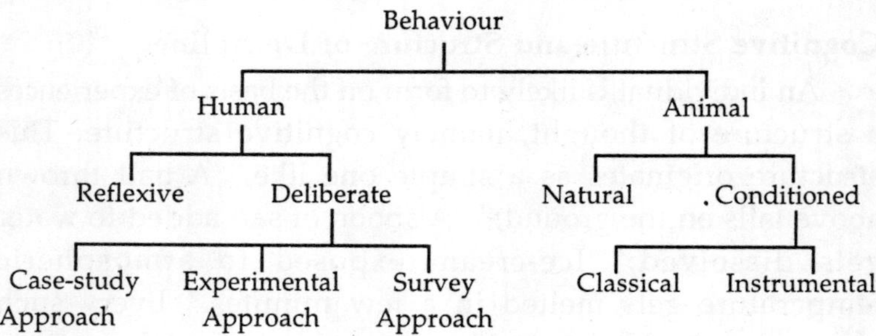

To sum up teaching in college or university can be markedly spruced and shaped by a training programme specially designed to meet the needs of adolescent and post-addolescent learners. The content must include Advanced Educational Psychology and Models of Teaching to perfect several techniques. One must learn how to conduct seminars, Tutorials and Quizz programmes. Unless it is made mandatory, most teachers might chose to miss this vital component of teaching.

63

Delayed and Immediate Feedback

Students need to be attentive in class to grasp whatever is taught and firmly register them in their memory. They have to retain and recall the same at the appropriate time. Usually a teacher presents a lesson sequentially in about nine or ten class-periods spread over two or three weeks. Soon after the completion of a lesson a test is conducted for students. Let us assume that the students have no difficulty in understanding the lesson and that the teacher has done his job well. Yet, the day before the test, all students make hectic preparation to revise or review all that they have learnt in class. They would abandon their usual play and recreation and spend time on reading.

While attending classes, students might have carefully taken notes as well. They might have understood and enjoyed the lesson. But seldom would they have bothered to consolidate what they had learnt by rehearsal and reinforcement at home. They might be under the impression that whatever they understood would be automatically stored in their memory for retrieval at a later date.

Very few of them are aware that memory is a "leaky bucket." Much of what we learn, somehow leaks out.

Rehearsing immediately or the same night as well as the following day is the only way by which the "holes" could be plugged and information retained. Most students tend to procrastinate and become vigilant only the day or a couple of days before the test. By that time the quantum of knowledge and information transacted in classes would have accumulated doubly. Quite naturally tension, anxiety and dilemma would mount up. A small experiment by the investigator with graduate students yielded favourable results.

The study was undertaken to examine the relative advantage of "Immediate feedback" over "Delayed feedback." Two units were taught in the conventional manner. Each unit required eight class periods spread over three weeks. Toward the end, a test was conducted to evaluate pupil performance. Even though every presentation was well received and understood by students, their performance in the Unit-test was not quite satisfactory. An alternative strategy was followed for the third unit. An outline of the lesson comprising eight sequential components was prepared and distributed to students. The class consisting of one hour was split thus: 25 minutes for teacher presentation, 15 minutes for clarification of doubts; 10 minutes for answering a short question in about 15 lines and 10 minutes for evaluation of their performance. The students were asked to exchange their test papers and were asked to grade thus: "Excellent, very good, good, and Not satisfactory." They were asked to comment briefly in addition to grading. The same procedure was followed for the remaining periods of teaching.

Soon after the completion of the unit a comprehensive test of one-hour duration was held similar to the ones taken for the earlier two units. There was a significant improvement in their standards in the Unit-test. Immediate feedback obtained in every instructional hour made the students more alert, involved, less tense and anxious and more enjoyable as well. Thus, one could combine teaching and evaluation to ensure optimum learning. There was a perceptible change in pupil-behaviour on the eve of the test under the modified teaching strategy. They were less tense, more relaxed and confident. All that is required of a teacher is adequate planning and able execution.

"Minds are like Parachutes. They only function when they are open"

—*Sir James Dewar.*

"Health is wealth-and it's tax free.

—*Arnold Glason.*

64

To Receive or to Discover?

Normally most class teachers impart knowledge to pupils by verbal narration. Whether it is science or social Studies, more time is spent in listening to the exposition of theories, principles and facts. The skill of the teacher lies in effective presentation that would counteract the tendency among pupils to be distracted or dissipated. The teacher might use the black-board, charts, models and also improvised situation to vivify instruction. However, he gains experience in developing a style of communication that would arrest in attention and facilitate concentration. We may call this mode of teaching Expository technique and the resultant learning as MEANINGFUL RECEPTION. DAVID AUSUBEL is an exponent of this mode of presentation.

Ausubel is of the view that, sooner on later, pupils will have to acquire knowledge through print-media and by self-learning. Verbal learning in unavoidable, particularly in higher stages. Pupils who have a strong base in vocabulary will have an edge over those who are deficient. Listening to a lecture binds the pupil and the teacher as every word is hooked into the cognitive structure of the pupils. Consequently the cognitive map of the pupils gets enlarged and enriched. Though pupils might seem to remain passive, they do not remain inactive. On the other hand they are actively assimilating every word and phrase and they do interrupt and seek clarification whenever they are puzzled. It becomes easier for them to share with their class-fellows what they had acquired through verbal communication. Hence verbal learning is not inherently ineffective.

Another school of thought propagates DISCOVERY LEARNING. JEROME S. BRUNER, an exponent of INDUCTIVE method of learning holds the view that real learning results from personal EXPERIENCE. A student has to perform .experiments, make shrewd guesses, reject inappropriate hypotheses, formulate principles, test their validity and then alone accept laws. In other words, a pupil plays the role of a scientist and learns to discover the way in which famous scientists arrived at knowledge. Bruner is emphatic that such training at school-level would lay the foundation of future learning. When once the pupils acquire the know-how it is easier for them to learn by themselves. Undoubtedly, motivation is of a higher order in such discovery-learning and accountability also in ensured. Teacher's role is to FACILITATE self-learning. It is easier said than done in the context of the swelling student-strength in class and also the expanding curricular matter year after year. There are merits in both modes of teaching. It is not fair to compare and contrast the two modes of teaching. A resourceful teacher can employ both methods at different levels and promote learning in class. It is better to avoid die-hard stance and believe only in verbal narration. It is equally indiscreet to swear by Discovery method-alone as the sole medium of instruction. A flexible approach is likely to generate pupil-involvement. The acid-test of teaching is increased pupil participation and motivation. Since both approaches do not eliminate this factor it is not all that difficult to harmonise the views of Ausubel and Bruner.

65

The Roots and Shoots of Science

What do we mean by "Education"? In broad terms "it is an attempt to assist everyone actualise potentialities to an optimum, if not maximum level. Inasmuch as one cannot eat for others, sleep for others, breathe for others, a teacher cannot do the 'Learning' on behalf of students. One has to experience' the process of learning to learn. A teacher could at best arrange situation in and around school that would facilitate learning learning by pupils. When we trace the history of any branch of science we could notice that it always originated in one's curiosity, eagerness and effort to unravel the inscrutable mysteries of the universe. Centuries of tireless efforts might have yielded a grain of truth. However, the quest has to continue because every conquest gives rise to further quest. The famous astronomer EDDINGTON compares man's position in the universe with that of a potato bug inside a potato inside a sack, placed in the basement of a ship, floating on the sea, trying to know what the sea is like. In the same way we are in this planet of a solar system, which is part of a galaxy and which is, in twin, a part of the system of galaxies in a small part of the universe, and we are trying to look through all these limitations what is beyond!

Most of the discoveries seem to be accidental. It may

appear so to an onlooker, but not always to a thinker. Before the discovery of 'Penicillin—a group of substances that stop the growth of bacteria—countless people died due to infection. ALEXANDER FLEMING must have been preoccupied with this problem for days and nights. What he accidentally found in a mould in a dish turned out to be formidable antibodies to fight the harmful bacteria that saved millions and billions of lives. Not for nothing ALFRED NOBEL bequeathed a fortune to those outstanding persons.

Just imagine the kind of darkness in which people had to grope before THOMAS ALVA EDISON came out with the filament called "Tungsten!" Did he not illumine the world by his discovery?

Despite being deaf GRAHAM BELL could bring the whole world to your drawing room by the invention of 'Telephone.' It has become so common that we seldom salute the genius who made it first.

The opaque human body was made transparent thanks to the discovery of the x-rays by RONTGEN! The bumping of the kettle lid energised the thinking of JAMES WATT that resulted in steam locomotive. The list is endless. What is common among these uncommon individuals is their power of observation, experimentation, verification and formulation of a theory. This is called Scientific thinking!

Let us examine the school curriculum with particular reference to science education. Teachers of science, right from primary grades, ought to prepare their lesson in such a manner that would always capitalise the inborn curiosity of children, In the hierarchy of teaching profession many might hanker after a position at the apex, leaving the thrill and excitement of working at the base. No matter how elegantly and comfortably you had designed the upper deck of the ship it is bound to sink if the keel is weak and leaky. No matter how cosy the upper storey is the multistoreyed mansion would collapse and cave in if adequate strength is not provided at the foundational stage. Similarly, no matter how sophisticated the equipment you provide a university laboratory with, no tangible outcome might emanate if you neglect the quality of teaching at the primary grade!

Aren't children baffled by the bewildering variety of things that surround them? Don't they pester parents and teachers with scores of queries—Why do birds fly, fish swim, worms crawl, dogs have four legs, horses run faster than bullocks, Sun rises in the East and sets in the West, leaves are green, flowers are red, water in a river flows in one direction, sea-water is salty, and it does not swallow the land and so on! Teachers could collect such innocuous, innocent questions and seek answers from the Encyclopaedia to prepare a FUNCTIONAL CURRICULUM. This could run parallel to the structured and standardised one followed at school. The purpose of collecting and collating such queries of kids is to enable them to learn to think, analyse and understand the world. Not that satisfactory answers could be found all the time. But, the process of SCIENTIFIC THINKING emerges. Children must feel that Science is not something imposed on them, but emanating from them! They must be made to feel that they have a right to use questions even though they may not always obtain right answers. They must be trained to follow scientific thinking to understand science—to be free from dogmas and superstitious beliefs.

Science is a way of living. It is to enable everyone to utilise God-given faculties of thinking and imagination. It is to make one realise that what baffled our ancestors no more baffle us because science has unravelled myriads of mysteries. To quote BENNETT:

"Scientific method involves the orderly
gathering of data by means of accurate
observations by trained personnel,
aided by precise instruments; the classifying
and organising of data on the basis of
similarities, variations, activities,
processes, causes, results, the application
of constructive imagination, discernment,
known principles to formulate tentative
generalisation; verifying these generalisations
by controlled experiments; submitting
the findings to those who are qualified
to criticise and interpret."

A scientist works far from the public glare in a laboratory far from the madding crowd to examine the flora fauna on this Good Earth, to experience the agony and ecstasy of quest, shorn of pride and prejudices; but he stoops to conquer not to remain a solitary reaper of all that he discovered or invented, but to leave a legacy for mankind to benefit.

"People remember God thrice;
When they are hatched
When they are matched and
When they are despatched."

— *Inge.*

66

Observational Learning or Modelling

Here is a startling news published in "the Hindu" (June 20, 1996) abut a youth. It sounds horrific and unbelievable.

"SASKATOON (CANADA): A 14-year old boy, influenced by a horror film he saw at least ten times, killed and skinned a young play-mate, then cooked his victim's flesh on a stove, the boy's lawyer told a court on Tuesday. The accounts from the defence lawyer .... and from prosecutors marked the first time that horrific details became public in a murder case that had been kept confidential upto now because of the age of the defendant, Sandy Charles.

Normally, youths under 18 are tried in the youth Court in Canada and their names cannot be made public. But, Charles, because of the nature of the case, was tried in adult court. According to the defence lawyer, Barry Singer, Charles was under the delusion after repeated viewings of the horror movie "War Lock" that he would be able to fly if he drank boiled fat from his victim, seven-year-old, Jonathan Thimpsen."

Around the mid-seventies, television came to India as media of entertainment. Within a quarter of a century, it has reached every nook and corner of our country. We have already begun to reap the harmful consequences of the "small screen." Seldom do we realise that by bringing in this "little monster"—the "Idiot-box"—into our drawing room, we have invited trouble. It is too tempting to be ignored.

Once upon a time, the drawing room of a house used to draw visitors who would engage the host in delectable conversation that would smoothen human relations! Nowadays visitors are unwelcome during the telecast of "Action Movies" or "Tele Serials" and those who chose to intrude, will have no option but to watch silently or leave the place quietly. T.V. predominates among the mass media available to young children. American children, we are told, watch TV for an average of 56 hours a week (averaging 8 hours per day) — more than they spend on any other activity except sleep. Physical violence occurs in 80% of the programmes. Cartoons sometimes figure more than violence. Indian kids are not far behind, what with the invasion of skies through the cable TV network, beaming cheap, sordid scenes round the clock. Reading habits have steadily declined. Everyone is glued to the small screen.

Children exposed to violent TV programmes tend to increase their aggressive behaviour. They begin to fight fiercely among themselves. A six-year investigation of 1565 adolescent boys in London revealed that boys who were shown to be habitual viewers of violent TV programmes tended to commit significantly more violent acts than those who did not. Quite a few crazy lads indulge in ugly eve-teasing, imitating their favourite villains in movies. Erotic scenes are included in such slapstick movies that rouse the passions of quite a few adolescents and adults to enact in real life what they witnessed in a world of fantasy. Permissivenes is carried to such ridiculous extremes that the chair-person of the Censor Board is coerced into approving such unwholesome entertainments. Children have an irrepressible urge, an unconscious tendency to identify themselves with the MODELS they view. They begin to IMITATE the violent behaviour in real life.

Pre-school children were brought individually into a playroom where another person (either another child or an adult model) was already engaged actively in aggressive play. As the children entered the room, they saw the model hitting doll, throwing and breaking objects in the room and employing aggressive language. Later, the children were brought to another room and allowed to play freely with any of the toys there. Some of the toys resembled those they had seen being used previously in an aggressive manner. In the second situation, however, no one was present to influence the children. The experimenter found that the play of children in this part of the experiment matched the aggressive behaviour of the model they had watched earlier.

Observing an aggressive model led to the acquisition of certain aggressive verbal and physical responses not previously found in them. It also led to the disinhibition of aggressive responses they had earlier learned to control. Those children who observed the aggressive model exhibited twice as many aggressive acts as the control children. On the other hand the children who observed the non-aggressive model exhibited significantly less aggression than the control group and thereby also testified to the potential inhibitory effects of observing certain types of behavior in a model.

ALBERT BANDURA, a Canadian Psychologist and his disciple, RICHARD WALTERS of England introduced the term MODELLING in their book titled "Social Learning and Personality Development," published in 1963. Later, Bandura wrote a book titled "Psychological Modelling," in 1971. It is a kind of imitative learning and Personality Development," published in 1963. Later, Bandura wrote a book titled

"Psychological Modelling" in 1971. It is a kind of imitative learning or "Observational Learning." Children in the classroom are imitative. The teacher serves as model. Social stimulation and imitative responding are involved in learning how to walk and talk in early life, apart from maturation. Social manners relating to greeting, thanks - giving, appreciating, eating, drinking, dressing are all learned through imitation. It is not just imitation of a performance model, but identification with a personal model.

In the classroom the teacher commands great respect. Every little gesture and speech of the teacher is unconsciously copied and admirably imitated by children. Every time children return home from school they will have something or other to share with parents. It may be as trivial as how the teacher wore her saree or walked or smiled or silenced them when they behaved naughtily. Children adore and respond to teachers who are demonstrably kind yet firm. The tend to dislike those who are harsh and who short at them. More aggressive teachers tended to have more aggressive students. When compared with children who have non-punitive teachers, children who have punitive teachers manifest more aggression in misconduct. These little observations leave an indelible impression upon tender minds and sow the seeds of attraction or aversion toward schooling.

Observational learning has an advantage over deliberate, conscious learning. When children attempt to learn anything deliberately, they experience a kind of pressure or compulsion. Even with regard to learning something quite simple children are likely to result instruction. But they would effortlessly learn to pronounce the word WORLD with the letter "r" silent or to say "you are welcome" when someone thank them. Quite often they are not even aware they are copying.

Bandura makes a distinction between learning and

performing. Learning, by and large, refers to such activities that are planned to produce deliberately such behaviours as are valuable and purposeful. There is an element of volition and also compulsion. On the other hand, performing is something that is VICARIOUS. It is a kind of experiential learning.

The physical Education teacher may demonstrate to students how to shoot a basket-ball into the ring, catch a cricket ball, how to hold the bat, how to swing the arm during pace-bowling and spin-bowling, and so on. He need not explain all these verbally. By observing the performance of a coach, players grasp the technique. Sometimes they would be surprised to find themselves performing perfectly even on the first trial. Hence imitation is termed by Bandura, "No trial learning."

Modelling is an effective technique to use with children to treat a variety of problems such as intense fear of snakes or dogs. Fearful individuals who have seen a model perform the behaviour they fear (e.g. petting a dog) without suffering any adverse effects reduce their efforts to avoid that behaviour.

Modelling is used in ASSERTIVENESS TRAINING. Some people get easily frightened and lack self-confidence. They can watch another person saying "No' or standing up for his rights without being annoyed or aggressive. The first step in assertiveness training is to encourage self-assertion. Later, the training involves a more detailed, systematic procedure including breaking down the problem into a series of more manageable segments. Each segment has a practical orientation and is well rehearsed before the client attempts an integrated behaviour-pattern.

Leaders observe films showing supervisors dealing effectively with certain critical situations. After discussing the principles that the model followed, the observers role-play the desired behaviours themselves and receive feedback from the group and trainer. Leaders who are trained in this manner show long-lasting improvements in their leadership skills when they return to their work-settings.

A 38-year-old Engineer felt depressed and demoralised as he held junior positions in his work although he had better qualifications. It was found by psychologists that the patient's difficulty was a gross difficulty in assertive behaviour. Modelling and imitation were used to train him in assertive behaviour at the office. In one session the patient was told that he was appearing for an interview with a prominent executive for a position. Therapist acts as an interviewer: "Come in!" he says:

The subject opens the door and hesitantly approaches the desk. The therapist interrupts and mirrors the subject's timid gestures, shuffling gait, downcast eyes and over-all tension.

The subject is asked to play the role of an Executive. The therapist enacts the patient's role. The patient is asked to criticise the patient's performance. Then the therapist models the entry of an assertive individual. The patient is asked to note the variations in posture, gait, voice, etc. Then he rehearses the whole thing. This promotes "assertiveness." It is repeated several times. Each interview is analysed. Several months later the patient got his promotion.

In short, modelling in an effective technique to mould the behaviour of students in a wholesome manner. At the same time, we need to ensure that they do not choose unworthy models of the celluloid world for imitation. We are compelled to wage a war with the advertising agencies and films that tempt the youth with wrong, fictitious models. The purpose of education is to help the students choose proper, worthy models for emulation.

67

Discovery Learning

Is it not unfortunate that in schools we have unwittingly or intentionally supported an attitude of acquiescence rather than robust skepticism? The Scientific temper among learners would get blunted by fostering a "taking-things-for-granted" tendency. Should a teacher misconstrue an intelligent searching query raised by a precocious student' over a time-honoured truth? Would Einstein or Raman be offended if a fertile brain were to find flaws in their discoveries? Are scientific truths eternally true? Are they immutable?

Why do we teach science in school? Science teachers are purportedly expected to foster independent, divergent thinking among pupils. JEROME S. BRUNER pleaded for promoting DISCOVERY LEARNING wherein stress was laid on INTUITIVE LEAPS in judgment and also freedom to make mistakes in conjectures. An insecure teacher would not venture beyond the prescribed text-book and would proscribe random gazing by zealous learners. What transpires in most class rooms is nothing but passive acceptance of what a text-book writer has doled out. Should we not grant children the democratic right of dissent?

Teachers generally desire to remain supreme and unapproachable. They consider it a blow to their reputation if a student were to find flaws in the enunciation of scientific truth. To conceal his incapacity to defend himself or the author of the text-book a teacher is likely to brand a promising student as impertinent, if not insolent. He would be politely told that his question would be answered in higher classes. In his wisdom, a teacher would consider it premature to accelerate cognitive development. An inquisitive learner confronted with such rebuff, prefers to remain quiet and passive. Wore still, he might be tempted to accept a palpable untruth as something too profound to be probed. In the long run his reasoning ability would atrophy due to disuse.

Have are a few Do's and Dont's for teachers:

(i) Support and encourage a questioning frame of mind among pupils.

(ii) Provide opportunities for re-examining an accepted theory.

(iii) Reward a student whenever he comes out with an innovative idea.

(iv) Allow passes while teaching so as to provide time to students to absorb what has been taught.

(v) Encourage interactive communication among students and be a bystander and not an intruder.

(vi) Accept the inability to answer an intelligent question when one is unable to answer.

(vii) Do not attempt to impose authority and stifle curiosity.

(viii) Do not swear by the text-book and pass on disorted contents.

(ix) Do not harass the students by a surfeit of recall and scanty application-level questions.

(x) Do not be anxious to complete the syllabus in a hurry.

68

The Art of Teaching

Any enduring behavioural change that cannot be ascribed to non-volitional activity but has been deliberately caused by systematic, well-planned instructional schedule within a time-frame could be termed "Learning" and the very process of effecting such a change upon an individual is termed "Teaching." Unlike a host of behavioural changes that could be attributed to incidental, informal learning, classroom learning is said to be more disciplined, goal directed and time-bound. Teachers in schools are saddled with the responsibility of simplifying and transmitting the contents of a Text-book in assimilable form to a heterogeneous group of learners.

A teacher needs to individualise instruction, make it meaningful to the majority of learners, attend to the needs of the mediocre and slow learners assess them periodically and also prepare them for the terminal public examination—all within the academic year. Ironically, in our social-set up educational institutions are easy targets to express public dissent for real or imaginary inequities and remain closed for weeks at a stretch. Teachers anticipate such eventualities as closure of schools and hence plan accordingly so that the least damage is caused to students' interests.

Generally teachers are meticulous in planning their

lessons and strive to deliver them to the best of their capacity. They are sufficiently prepared to clarify doubts and answer the bewildering questions in the class. This preparedness and earnestness provide satisfaction to the students and self-fulfilment to the teachers. After all he is given a limited time to teach an unlimited content, not always under congenial conditions. At least during the initial days of his career a teacher tends to be painstaking in his preparation so as to earn a good name among his students and parents. Every succeeding year he experiences a gradual increase in his mastery of content and pedagogy. One cannot rest on his oars and allow complacency to set in. The initial thrust and drive must be kept up to maintain the momentum all through his career.

We come across a variety of designations such as Teachers, Lecturers and Professors even though everyone is supposed to "teach." It is more or less in a pyramidal form with teachers occupying the base, and providing a solid and firm foundation and support. In a lighter vein it may be remarked that a teacher teaches, a lecturer lectures and a professor professes!

The act of teaching is the common denominator meaning thereby, a carefully designed mode of instruction and transmission of knowledge that would germinate and take roots in the minds of learners so as to enable them to mature and discover knowledge by self-effort. Such a feat cannot be achieved by youngsters without proper tutoring and monitoring by the perceptors. It is an illusion or perhaps an alibi put forth by preceptors in higher education that students could fend for themselves with minimal stimulation.

Post-graduation and Doctoral studies provide a solid content-base with the strength of which a lecturer embarks on his teaching career. The thrill and excitement of addressing a gathering of adolescents and the cultivation of fluency provide immense joy to a novice in a college. He has a syllabus, if not a Textbook, to go by and a host of reference materials for gathering information. He has to be well-informed to locate where the requisite information is available. Any attempt on his part to bestow disproportionate attention upon ornamental language at the expense of sound content would not be welcomed by serious-minded students.

The dynamics of a high-school classroom with all the Question-answer sessions and Activity-based teaching seem to be conspicuously missing and substituted by a sort of impersonality if not non-accountability. The higher one ascends in the hierarchy of higher education, the less one gets involved in the business of imparting instruction.

Most students are left high and dry after a mesmerising monologue in the lecture-halls. Under the garb of student-initiative for self-study many a teacher would avoid undue effort and strain. However, if this is deliberately planned, fostered and supervised so as to instil such traits like self-reliance, critical-mindedness and self-discovery it is praiseworthy. On the other hand, if it is an offshoot of dereliction and wilful neglect, it is likely to breed unhealthy attitudes among students. The simmering discontent among students may be partially attributed to the ham-handed treatment meted out to them in class.

Those engaged in higher education must replenish knowledge by reading new Text-books and periodicals. Never should one appear before a class without doing adequate homework regardless of the experience gained over the years. Every year of teaching must add some new insight to the repertoire of his teaching skills and quantum of knowledge. Never should one take his students for a ride and indulge in verbalism. Teachers at the collegiate level face inadequate time to cover a vast syllabus and hence they need to budget time adequately.

An outline of the course-content could be prepared by spelling out the major objectives and specific ones and allocating time for teaching, group-work, and evaluation. Exhaustive references could be provided for supplementary reading. If this could be handed over to students during the first meeting session they tend to bestow a little more seriousness in class. It also checks the temptation of teachers to digress and waste precious time. One should not take students for granted; rather students are granted to a teacher to educate!

> "Alas! It is not till time, with reckless hand, has torn out half the leaves from the book of human life, to light the fires of passion with, from day to day, that man begins to see that the leaves which remain are few in number'
>
> — *Longfellow.*

69

Allow a Child to be a Child!

None receives a better VIP treatment than the new-born! It is a perennial source of joy to parents and almost to everyone in the household. The tiny creature that remained supine and somnolent and encased within the protected prenatal environment of mother's womb for several months starts kicking, crying, gazing and sucking that is indeed rapturous to the mother. Caressed and constantly kissed by everyone, the little one is seldom left alone. The mother swells with pride at her new acquisition, particularly when she is blessed with one after several years of penance to the creator! Its silken hair and fluffy frame are pleasant to stroke. It demands the exclusive attention of everyone. It is being passed on from person to person and disturbed even while at sleep! The cradle ceremony is an important event at home, with ladies in their rustling silk sarees, visiting and blessing the mother and her treasure-hunt. It is rocked and entertained with lullabies improvised for the occasion.

Most babies smile and acknowledge all such extravaganza whole-heartedly though a few might squirm and feel ill-at-ease in the presence of unfamiliar faces. How long would this last? May be a few weeks or months perhaps. Babies do grow and develop and also mature gradually. These need an enriched, balanced diet though, of course, in liquid form at regular intervals. If some babies do not respond to such feeding the grandmother at home would attribute this negativism to the casting of "evil eyes" by some jealous ladies who were not blessed with babies!

Alas, so ephemeral is the ecstasy of infancy that the little creature that demanded the undivided attention of every one is demanded to pay undivided attention to what his teacher says in class! Yes. Infanticide takes place in classrooms. Innocent, innocuous kids are dressed up and whisked off to schools, to be "educated." The transition could be traumatic.

The symbiotic union with the mother is torn asunder. Young ones with tear soaked cheeks would be delivered at the door steps of schools to receive 'knowledge.' There might even be feverish rehearsals to fare well before the school board to gain admission. Endless repetition of the letters of the alphabet, days of the week, months and the year and related 'mumbo'-'jumbo' would have been stuffed into the tiny heads by over-zealous mothers, hell-bent on admitting children into prestigious prep schools. Why cannot we allow a child to be a child? Why should we make him smarter than he need be? Why do we fast-forward the cassette?

Most kids cry, cry and cry and finally reconcile themselves to the inevitable separation, to be in the company of fellow-sufferers. Each child is an island into itself first and only gradually canals are dug to join islands and make a lake. What will the poor teacher do with a flock of untamed creatures, challenging her forbearance every second for days and weeks! The little ones would move around like puppies and flap around like dragon flies and sleep too like tired calf! A teacher is not a baby-sitter. Nor a priest to demand submission and devotion. Not at all a ringmaster to flog kids to perform miraculous mental gymnastics! He/she needs to "understand" a child and allow him to grow naturally, spontaneously and joyously too! Anything taught and learnt under regimentation or coercion tends to breed aversion and derision. In as such as it is foolish to accelerate the blossoming of bud into flower, it is far from prudent to drive kids to ascend the cognitive hillock in rapid strides. Worse still to burden these creatures with a knapsack of books and note books to be transported to school and back. Should they stoop to conquer? Can't we conceive of a system wherein children go to school empty-handed, free and happy, collect their kits from their lockers in the class, do whatever they need to do and wish to do only in class and leave the school, gay and happy. Any parent who is inquisitive to know what is happening to their children at school could visit by prior appointment, to know the accomplishment of children.

Can't children divide their time to work, play and rest- each done in equal sincerity. Overemphasis on scholastic work tends to cause anxiety and aversion Play can mitigate the harmful influence of verbalism and memorisation. Heavens will not fall if a child does not count up to hundred effortlessly, does not distinguish morning from evening or even the classification of matter into liquid, solid and gas! He would learn, certainly learn, if only you free him from the dirty practice of reward and punishment. Why should we reward and why at all should be punish? Most things are learnt informally in class. Take children out, let them see their shadows shrinking and stretching and also disappearing at different times and draw their own inferences. Let them feel the grass, the petals of flowers the, stem of different plants, collect butterflies, watch caterpillars, frogs, earth worms and let them, on their own absorb whatever they wish to absorb. Do not give them a test immediately upon their return to record their observations classify, label and all that. Charles Darwin was 'not tormented by overzealous teachers!

Teach them music if they wish. For Heaven's sake do

not goad them to exercise their vocal chords at odd hours in chorus. Before teaching them their school prayer or National Anthem, tell them what these mean, if you know. Show them disarranged books and arranged books in the library; Ill-arranged and well-arranged furniture; ill-dressed and well dressed children drawn up on a board, short-tempered and even-tempered behaviours in a mock play, the effect of balanced diet and imbalanced diet upon health by showing illustrative cartoon—and leave the choice to children. You do not choose for them!

Let them begin a day with a question and end it with a question. Instead of asking them to do home work, you answer their queries. Let them grade you as 'good' 'bad' or indifferent Remember, children are 'God's creations. Do not deflect this development with a strait jacketed curriculum. Renew and recast the curriculum every year for every class, for every child. Reinforce in them the belief that you CARE for them for what they ARE and not what they "ought" to be. After all every one gets only one chance in life to be an infant and a child. Adult-cares can wait, because it is much longer than childhood. Give then a good start and let them glide happily, merrily. In short, allow child to be a child!

70

Do We Teach or Coach?

I called on a colleague of mine who has retired from teaching in a college of repute. Knew him for several years. He is an indefatigable conscientious teacher. To him this retirement was a punishment as he found time hanging heavily upon him. Having been conditioned to teach graduate as well as post-graduate classes almost every day, he felt he was under house-arrest. He didn't know how to spend the ample time he had now. He received substantial retirement benefits. His sons were well settled. Hence, there was no compulsion to seek part-time or full-time job. He could now relax, take life easy, let time pass without compunction, read newspaper and magazines of all kinds leisurely. Some habits die hard, especially study-habits. He found reading magazines rather frivolous and futile. He had distanced himself from politics so much that he was even ignorant of the Governor of the state wherein he lived. But, he could remember and rejoice over the discovery of Raman-effect or Archimedes Principle or Marie Curie's discovery of radium! His passion for Physics was enormous!

At the college he served he earned name as an outstanding teacher. Students yearned to learn from him, they did not learn merely to earn! He was fully accountable and loyal to the institution that paid him a decent salary. He was contented. He did not succumb to the temptation of coaching students through private tuition. Students used to meet him beyond class-hours for clarification. He used to be at his desk precisely by four—O'clock every morning to prepare for his classes. At six, he would be out for jogging or walking. Students would find him either in the laboratory or library whenever he had no class. Precisely by five in the evening he would be found in the Tennis Court to play vigorously till twilight. Back at his desk by nine O'clock at night he would go through student's assignments/test-paper/record books and so on. He never needed sleeping pills!

Now he was face to face with retirement. A clock doesn't retire, nor does the human heart or mind. Water always flows along the river and never do we see a sea without waves. Rest results in rust. He was restless. To break the tyranny of monotonous idleness he decided to teach students at home. Quite a few colleges and schools were around his locality. He announced through local newspapers and also put up a small board at the entrance of his house: TUITIONS UNDERTAKEN.

The message percolated. Quite a few students approached him and enrolled for tuition. Anyway he was not a "Professional" tutor or "Coach," but just a classroom teacher. He declared to the newcomers that his main objective was to explain, elucidate some of the concepts in Physics that might pose difficulties to them. He began in all earnestness, dwelt at length upon the pioneers in Physics like C.V. Raman, Chandrasekar, Newton, Faradey Einstein, Edison and gradually introduced some of the living great scientists like Jayant Narlikar, M.G.K. Menon, D. Balasubramanian, Raja Ramanna and so on. He thought he could magnetise students by teaching "Electricity and Magnetism." Soon he realised that there was a power shut-down in the minds of students. He could notice palpable indifference and impatience in their faces.

One day they plainly and unabashedly told him that all that they needed was "Notes" and "Answers" and not lessons! To the teacher it was like putting the cart before the horse! How could one frame questions or answer questions before learning a subject? He felt that it would be foolhardiness to convert Physics into a "Question-answer format'—to be memorised blindly and regurgitated in examination. Students started dropping out one by one. Finally he was left with very few students who came to study Physics and not answers to questions.

Across the road a roaring business of coaching was in full swing. Plenty of cycles, mopeds, scooters and even four-wheelers were parked in front of the house in the mornings and evenings, blocking vehicular traffic. There was brisk sale of knowledge! It picked up during examination times! The humble teacher in the house never exerted himself at the school he worked. At home, he would work like hell, to offer private tuition. He had enough patience and perseverance. He had mastered the "Art." Otherwise, how could he put in eight solid hours by way of private tuition plus eight "semi-solid" hours of teaching at school! Don't ask me what happens in tuition class. That is top secret!

71

Improving Homework: Some Suggestions

If a referendum were to be held to elicit the views of students to identify the most detestable aspect of schooling, an overwhelming majority would simply scream "Down with Homework." So sickening has become this work! Few teachers would give up this pernicious practice because it has been an integral part of education since times immemorial. It is not that easy to abolish it. How many of the teachers will admit honestly their superficial correction of homework turned in by an assortment of learners day in and day out? Of course, most students cleverly conceal their poor work by neat handwriting. It pays. A good number simply copy religiously from books or from the notebooks of classmates. Only a teacher with a forensic capacity can identify the "copywriters" from the original! Still he would be at his wit's end to decide who is who!

A home with a few school going children presents a sorry spectacle during evening hours and this would extend till late hours at night. Excessive tension and a sense of pressure are invariably, associated with homework. Both parents and teachers demand from youngsters a monastic devotion to academic pursuits, particularly home assignments. Television is shut off. Visitors are unwelcome and a solemn silence in maintained to create the "conducive atmosphere" for completion of homework. Even nursery school kids are not spared of this ordeal! The mother or the father would breathe down the necks of these poor creatures while they copy what they should copy, neatly, legibly and correctly. Mistakes are bound to creep in under such vigilant supervision. Using a poor quality eraser, the child would make smudges, that would invite generous dosage of rebukes. Tear glands of children would work overtime during homework!

When children are grown up they are relatively free from such constant vigil. Yet they receive signals to stop playing and start working. They must finish a certain quota before supper and complete the rest before they go to bed. Homework appears to be more of an exercise to the wrist muscles than brainwork. Starving the brain and straining the brawn is not praiseworthy. It is an euphemism to call it homework, because it is, infact, school work done at home.

Morning time at most homes would present a kind of frenzied activity very much resembling the quick-motion movies of the Charlie Chaplin era. Little angels will have to bathe, dress, eat breakfast, wear uniform, ties, socks and shoes before the school van arrives. Stuffing a dozen note books, textbooks, crayons, lunch box and water bottle in haste into the school bag, these butterflies would wave "Ta Ta" to proud parents while boarding the school-van. An uneasy calm would descend at home almost like a long-distance train left the platform. The housewife would heave a sigh of relief. If the wife also is a working mother she would certainly get worked up as she has to get ready for her school or college!

For mental health, children and young people need to engage in worthwhile out-of-school tasks suited to their individual capacities. Homework should supply such tasks and reasonable freedom in carrying them out. Flexibility in the kind of asisgnment must replace unformity, with the objective of developing voluntary effort, initiative, responsibility and self-direction in the students. Whenever homework shuts out social experiences, outdoor recreation, and creative activities and whenever it usurps time that should be devoted to sleep, it is not meeting the basic needs of children and adolescents. The home conditions may be crowded so as to prevent privacy for study or even a place for spreading out books and papers. At times children need proper guidance to do their homework. Mother, who is busy in the kitchen, might pass the buck to her beloved partner who might have buried his face in the latest "Frontline" or "India Today." He would invariably misguide, only to receive a dressing down from his better-half later. When the parents are not in a position to give competent guidance, the student is likely to become confused, and even parents who are academically capable are likely to be emotionally so involved with their children that they make tense task-masters!

First and foremost both teachers and parents must give up their "mind-set" that children should be disciplined through homework. Any kind of discipline that is likely to create an aversive reaction is not worthwhile. We speak of "life-oriented education' these days. Grown-up children are expected to help parents in a variety of home-related tasks. Would it not be a nice idea to ask children to prepare a write-up on the kind of assistance they rendered to parents at home? Does it not improve their linguistic ability besides preparing them for life?

Why should the Television be taboo, particularly when some useful programmes are telecast! Teachers could give an assignment to children to prepare a write-up on a comic or cartoon they had watched on the TV or about some rare reptiles or animals shown in Discovery channel or National Geographic Channel or a review of the Turning Point programme. Would not such an assignment be really an exciting project to children and even reform parents who might otherwise switch on a slapstick show or some sentimental rubbish serial? Idiot-boxes can be converted into intelligent boxes if only we knew what to watch and what to be avoided.

Week-ends should be real week-ends-to relax and to rewind oneself for the Monday working day. Are not teachers too entitled to a little freedom from the routine of correction-work so that they could pursue some hobby other than school-related work? They could plan a field trip on an afternoon with a few students just to sing, dance and socials so that children could count on them as friends than sermonisers.' In the classroom too it is not necessary for teachers to exhaust themselves, teaching and teaching all the time. The attention-span of children is limited to a few minutes. Teaching should be dovetailed to testing in a non-threatening manner. Children will not demand teachers to sign the comprehensive Test Ban Treaty (CTBT) if only evaluation is left to students themselves. Teacher could work out the sum on the blackboard or write the model answer and ask children to exchange note books among classmates for correction This kind of immediate reinforcement helps students to be attentive and alert all the time in class and relieve them of the burden of homework. Teacher does not remain a passive spectator. He turns into a facilitator of learning, monitoring and guiding students as they are engaged in activity. Every student, regardless of his capacity, ought to be made to feel positive and not harbour negative self-image. The smarter ones should not be permitted to look down upon their less smart colleagues, but help them in all possible ways. Such a freedom granted to students would foster self-reliance and accountability

Grading is a degrading practice, more to stigmatise the slow learners than reward the fittest. It would be a healthy practice to stop marking students, instituting a kind of rat race in class that invariably breeds ill-will, jealousy and a kind of supercilious attitude among a few! The heart-burning of parents can be mitigated. Parents need counselling in this regard. Initially they might react unfavourably and misconsture such innovations as gimmicks to camouflage dereliction of duty.

Teachers must always think of assigning a kind of homework that would be creative and supportive to school-work. Students should look back with nostalgia their memorable school-days and cherish these activities assigned by "uncommon" teachers that lead to self-actualisation. We find the couplet in railway compartments.

> "Less Luggage More comfort, Make Travel a Pleasure." Why cant we adopt a similar maxim? "Less homework, more classwork, make schooling a pleasure!"

72

To be or Not to be in the Limelight

Everyone has to choose an avenue of life that suits him / her best. Landing in a job that merely offers better pay and perquisites world certainly be alluring though not always fulfilling. An average person might jump at it, if and when such an offer is made. However, those above average would not take a plunge, perhaps they would think twice before reacting in a reflex manner. Rather, they would reflect upon the offer, weigh the pros and cons and take a mature decision. They would not mind turning down an attractive offer. What could be the reason? Several conjectures can be made.

First and foremost, one must make a little introspection, analyse one's abilities and aspirations, endowments and ambitions, short-term and long-term gains, above all consider one's philosophy of life. 'X' might be happy with a well-paid job, but 'Y' may not like to be in it. Teaching is a vocation that does not seem to attract the best of brains despite considerable hike in pay package. It is perhaps a blessing in disguise. One endowed with a superior intellect might perhaps find it difficult to come down to the level of the average and below average. He might find the job dull and dreary. One needs infinite patience to teach the mediocre students, particularly those reluctant rebels who are attending school more out of compulsion/coercion them out of volition. One with a moderate intellect can empathise with the mediocre and make learning less stressful and more easy.

Those who are temperamentally attuned to be always in the limelight, receive accolades for adventurous action, socialise a lot, friendly with all and sundry and enormously extroverted, might find teaching not at all rewarding.

A teacher, if he is really a teacher, functions mostly within the four walls of a class room. He has a specific discipline to teach, a syllabus and a framework to complete. He has to teach not only a subject but also subjects whom he should teach. He finds fulfilment in the job and always projects his students to be in the limelight. He prefers to be in the background and is happy to push his students to the foreground. Therefore, anyone desirous of choosing the teaching profession must seriously ponder whether he/she would be willing to occupy a subordinate position.

This holds good even in the case of the principal of a school. A principled principal would not hanker after publicity and self-glorification. He is only a leader of the team, consisting of well-informed teachers. He transfers all the credits to his colleagues. Whenever he conducts staff meetings he talks less and listens to his colleagues. There is no feeling of hierarchy. Teachers feel they are working with the principal than under him. Such a climate is conducive to effective teaching-learning process. To assume that the leader has to lead always and others have to follow sheepishly is an anachronism.

Some of the management techniques like Brainstorming and synectics are equally valid in a teaching institution as well. Brainstorming is a management technique introduced by OSBORNE in the field of Industry. It can be used to promote "fluency of ideas." The participants are encouraged to produce as many ideas as they can, to solve a problem. Quantity begets quality. All criticisms and judgements are deferred, if not discouraged. Evaluation comes later at the time of termination of the session. Ideas should be expressed with brevity, clarity and specificity. Here people drop their defensiveness. Instead of competing for power and status, they compete for excellence and creativity of their ideas. Brainstorming reinforces a sense of participation.

Synectics, which means "fitting together diverse elements" was evolved by an American, William J.J. Gordon. It was first used in consumer industry. Normally an individual feels threatened by anything strange and attempt to force it into some acceptable, traditional pattern. Here we use the technique of "making the strange familiar." Then the individuals are advised to distance themselves from the problem by making the familiar strange." The question is to be viewed from new perspective. e.g. creating a wheelchair that can climb stairs, elimination of hostility between ethnic groups at lower levels in a department store.

In short, the leader has to practise democratic 'discussion rather than authoritarian domination. So long one does not have an obsession to be always in the limelight one would indeed be a light-house to show directions to all.

73

Blessings and Curses

> "The optimist sees the rose and not its thorns, the pessimist stares at the thorns, oblivious of the rose."
>
> —Kahlil Gibran

Most of us do not count our blessings, although seldom do we forget to enumerate our losses and sufferings. Thus, we have made life as miserable as possible. We have an inexhaustible list of shortages: living space, water, food-grains, pollution free atmosphere, social harmony, escalated cost of living coupled with inadequate earning powers. For a moment, why not count our blessings instead?

The resplendent Sun-God works all the time in both hemispheres every day, shedding abundant light, free of cost, to prince as well as pauper! Does not cloudy weather create depression, slow down plant-growth and dull our enthusiasm. Sun is a natural drier we badly need every day to dry clothes, reinforce brick and mortar during a building construction. Do we have a substitute for sun in case Sun-God went on leave? Think!

Precious water is plentily available absolutely free. If some Agency has chosen to store and supply water in limited quantities, whom are we to blame? It is just a demand-supply phenomenon. We are pretty demanding. Have we not proliferated human population far in excess of the free supply of Natural Resources? We curse everything else except ourselves! Rivers carry pure, uncontaminated water all over the land silently, unobtrusively, generously and unceasingly. We discharge dirty effluents, bathe ourselves as well as the cows and buffaloes, make it muddy and nasty. We contemplate on purifying water after upsetting the ecology!

We cannot create water in the laboratory to meet all our needs. But God does it in his natural laboratory installed all over the world absolutely free of cost. Do we care to thank the Almighty for His merciful gesture?

Our lives are brightened or darkened, enriched or impoverished by the kind of "attitudes" we bestow toward our fellow-human beings, the variegated "interests" that we cultivate, and above all the "values" we have imbibed and cherished. Among life's greatest blessings are LOVE, HOPE and TRUST—to help us do the things we `should' as well as we `must. LOVE like a smile, when it is given away can lighten a burden on brighten a day; HOPE, like a candle, whose comforting light is a guiding hand—a lamp in the night, TRUST, like faith, that with each day's dream more joys will appear, more cares will be gone. "Have the coverage to take your own thoughts seriously, for they will shape you," said Einstein!

We breathe all through day and night and there is not an inch of space where free supply of oxygen is not available! We may be able to produce oxygen in the laboratory and fill the same in a cylinder, to be used in the intensive care unit by patients battling for life. At what cost! Has not God cared intensively for every one of us? Think for a while the fate, of humanity when there is a paucity of oxygen. We take this for granted and do not realise the munificence of the Almighty!

We sow a seed on the soil, water it regularly so that it might germinate, grow into a plant that would give us vegetables and fruits! The soil is not our creation. We are not directly responsible for the plant-growth.

Someone above decides and determines. If only we were to recognise that invisible Supreme Being who guides us all the time, we would count our Blessings more than the curses!

Just imagine yourself to be in the place of HELEN KELLER! How would you have lived your life? Did not the great lady teach all of us a lesson? she says:

"I who am blind, can give one hint
to those who see; Use your eyes
as if tomorrow you would be
stricken blind. And the same method
can be applied to the other senses.
Hear the music of voices, the song
of a bird, the mighty strains of
an orchestra as if you would be
stricken deaf tomorrow. Touch
each object you want to touch
as if tomorrow your tactile sense
would fail. Smell the perfume of
flowers, taste with relish each
morsel as if tomorrow you could
never taste and smell again!
Glory in all the facets of
pleasure and beauty, which the
world reveals to you; make the
most of every sense!"

Most of us seem to be "severely handicapped" in life,

compared to the lady with an indomitable "Will like HELEN KELLER! Real happiness in absolutely free. Yet, how dearly we pay for its counterfeit! A flower-seller does not charge you when you inhale the fragrance of jasmine. Does it not pass through your nostrils to your heart and soul! Why don't you greet the rising golden Sun at the Eastern horizon every morning and bid farewell in the evening to the setting Sun at the Western Horizon? You don't have to be a Wordsworth to compose a sonnet but can't you be human enough to enjoy "Nature at its Best!" Enjoy good music, feel the petals of flowers, allow yourself to be treated to the enchanting chorus-singing of parrots as they return to their nests at dusk! We need a Helen Keller to tell us how to enjoy life and living! Listen to JOYCE KILMORE.

"I think that I shall never see
A poem as lovely as a tree
A tree whose hungry mouth is prest
Against the earth's sweet flowing breast
A tree that looks at God all day
And lifts her leafy arms to pray.
Poems are made by fools like me
But only God can make a tree."

We accumulate money in the Bank with great care, by thousands of acts of sacrifice, saving on this item and that, spending less and earning more. But a day comes when we have to lose the pile and go empty handed! But, there is another Bank, which receives deposits and maintains accounts strictly and confidentially. Every little sum is entered and accounted for — deeds, thoughts, and words good, bad and indifferent. No son can sue for that AASTHI (Property), no tax-gatherer can lay hands on it. No crook can transfer it to his purpose. Open a deposit account there in that Bank. The assets of the meritorious activities of previous births can be drawn upon now. Overdrafts are also possible. It is called the grace of God. It is conferred when you have earned it by good deeds, good thoughts, good feelings, good company and constant repetition and recollection of the name of God. Just as you keep your valuables in safe deposit vaults, surrender your jewels of intelligence, cleverness, capacity to serve and the gem that you value most, your Ego to the care of God. Then, you can be perfectly happy.

Religion is like an anchor that preserves our equilibrium when tossed by forces beyond our control. Apostles of religion—Jesus Christ, Gouthama Buddha, Mahavira Shankaracharya, Ramanujacharya, Madhwacharya, Prophet Mohammad taught us the virtue of detached attachment. None of them studied science that we know of. But, they practised the science of living. Science can neither analyse the essence of religious experience nor can analyse poetry or human love.

"If any little word of mine
may make a life brighter
If any little song of mine
may make a heart the lighter
God, help me speak the little word
and take my bit of singing
And drop it in some lovely vale
to set the echoes ringing
If any little love of music
may make a life the sweeter
If any little care of mine
may make a friend's the fleeter
If any little lift of mine
may ease the burden of another
God, give me love and care and strength
to help my toiling brother.

74

Stress and Mental Health

This is an age of anxiety. Industrialisation and urbanisation have generated competition, resulting in pressure, insecurity and stress. 'Wants' have outstripped 'needs', causing stress as well as distress. Tranquil 'life of the rural surroundings has given place to the tense, impersonal life of the metropolis.

We have become 'cogs' in the wheel of the industrialised world as Bertrand Russell put it. The symptoms of stress is a kind of restlessness, apathy and despair and marked diminution of Zest and Zeal, characteristic of a healthy person. Inadequate personal communication can compel an individual to bottle up his feelings and emotions that would generate stress. A sense of false pride stands in the way of plain-speaking. One is tempted to assume a facade that conceals inward insecurity. The age-old habit of crying over our agony upon the shoulders of an understanding companion has a cathartic effect. Surprisingly, this healthy outlet is sealed by the so-called sophistication characteristic of modern life. The net effect is accumulation of minor irritants that add upto unmanageable stress. With the invasion of the Idiot-box into the drawing room modern man is glued to the gadget, to experience vicarious satisfaction that can also cause frustration.

Stress has a marked debilitating effect upon the heart

muscles and the circulatory system. As the brain receives a "stress-message," the relevant nerve cells immediately act to stimulate the pituitary gland. The organ then activates other glands to secrete hormones, especially adrenaline, which is the substance that excites various bodily systems, including the heart. Immediately there are increases in systolic blood-pressure, heart-rate and pulse-pressure. Walter Cannon describes these physiological stress reactions as preparatory to `flight' or `fight'. The heart is working overtime to get blood around the body to those tensed muscles and the faster it pumps the greater the pressure exerted on the arteries. If the stress subsides, these responses die away. The body can be released from the tensions, to return to a state of equilibrium.

What happens to someone who is constantly in a condition of "high-stress"? Instead of returning to that desirable post-stress phase, the body `adapts" to the pressure so that the `fight' or `flight' changes in physiological response become a permanent feature. High blood pressure, constricted blood vessels, a pounding heart and exceptional circulation start to take over. We reach a critical point, which, a leading British cardiologist Dr. Peter Nixon has identified as the "Exhaustion curve." This leads to stress-induced heart-attack.

How does psychological functioning change under stress? At lower levels of stress, vigilance and alertness are increased and performance is often facilitated. Reaction is quicker and more certain, perception more discriminating, learning and memory more effective. At more intense levels or when coping mechanisms are weaker, psychological performance deteriorates. Precise motor skills are impaired, discrimination and judgment are more inaccurate, learning in slower, memory is less efficient and intellectual problem-solving is less effective.

Is a certain amount of stress desirable? Yes. The most effective functioning of mind occurs at an optimum and not a minimum level of stress. Without a level of optimum stress complacency develops. People normally work under pressure—with set target dates and deadlines. Psychologically healthy persons seek challenge and excitement and prefer to deal with manageable stress. When the limit exceeds, it endangers a person.

Imagine the situations where there are no deadlines for the tasks to be completed, no monitoring agency to ensure promptness. Laziness and delay would set in. At the same time when employees overstretch themselves, hyper-tension takes place. The former is called ROOS — Rust out stress syndrome; and the latter is called BOSS-burn out stress syndrome. Both are bad. Optimum stress infuses challenge and creates meaning and purpose to human life.

What is the relationship between personality and stress? Dr. Ray Rosemann and Dr. Meyer Friedman, two cardiologists indicated that coronary-prone people were what they called "Type-A" Personalities—driving competitive, obsessive, aggressive characters who are typical "workholics," always in a hurry in office, at home or in a restaurant! In contrast to the clock-watching "Type-A" person is the "Type-B" person, who is easy going, relaxed, ready to take time off to do very little, choosing to walk leisurely them jog or run in rapid strides, who can enjoy good music than watching an action-movie and who is not really interested in keeping up with Joneses or anyone else.

We get inspiration from Lord Vinayaka, who teaches us "Stress-management." "How could you remain unperturbed throughout your writing of the entire "slokas" of Mahabharatha" asked Ved Vyas to Lord Ganesha. The God replied, "I am like that thread in "Deepam." Irrespective of the level of oil, it burns steadily!

The message is that happiness in compared to the high level of oil and low level of sorrow. The stability under pressure is being preached by Him, which is the essence of stress management. That is what is exactly preached by Lord Krishna in Bhagavad Gita—STHITHA PRAGNYA—the person being unaffected under pressure. For that person, the pursuit of goal is more gratifying than the goal itself. For him, success is not a destination but a journey throughout.

Here are a few guidelines to reduce stress:

(i) Avoid getting overtired, by keeping a nice balance between rest and activity.

(ii) Make sure that you give yourself the time, conditions and frame of mind to ensure good enough, good quality sleep.

(iii) Cultivate the ability to say "No" to demands put on you if you feel that these are going to cause you to feel overburdened.

(iv) Don't be afraid to admit your limitations. We all have them, but only you can decide in all honesty where your own limits lie.

(v) Keep a "stress diary" in which you note your particularly stress times during the week. By spotting the critical periods you will be able to apply anti-tension-relaxation measures when they are needed to reduce your unwanted responses.

(vi) Never be shy about seeking help and advice about stressful situations. One of the problems with stress is that it can be self-reinforcing.

"Stress is like electric power.
It can make a bulb light-up,
and provide bright illumination.
However, if the voltage is higher
than what the bulb can take, it
can burn out the bulb!"

75

Great Expectations, Hard Times

Every time I watch programmes like KAUN BANEGA CROREPATI in T.V. channel I would wonder at the incredible pace with which one could become a millionaire. After all the Quiz is not all that challenging, certainly unrelated to the bonanza one could notch in a jiffy. Quite a few youngsters and elders would get tempted to amass a fortune without much labour and sweat!

On similar lines the astronomical rise in shares of some software giants, pushing down to the abysmal bottom most of the manufacturing industries of repute would give wrong signals to the people at large to indulge in speculation and hit the jackpot! Should I pity or look down upon the multitude of professionals or blue collared workers who toil for a minimum of eight hours a day only to receive a fraction of the compensation garnered through clever means listed above? What is the value of wealth, anyway?

Almost all through the year in all areas of a city we find road-diggers, masons working at a construction-site, gardeners, cobblers as well as vegetable vedors labouring long hours in rain or shine, to earn a few chips to keep the pot boiling at home! Their needs are met, but they are neither needy nor greedy like the speculators!

Going further down the memory-lane I recall the years of sweat and single-minded devotion of some distinguished personalities of bygone days. It was a struggle for survival!

The celebrated novelist, Charles Dickens had real "Hard Times" during his childhood days. Born and brought up under poverty in England, son of a minor clerk in the Navy Post-Office at the beginning of the Nineteenth Century, young Dickens' childhood was spent under the shadow of economic insecurity. His father had to be lodged in the debtor's prison and his mother with four of her children went to join her husband in prison. Young Charles was an orphan, eking out his livelihood at a blacking factory for six shillings a week, sticking labels on pots. Those few months were for Dickens a time of utter misery, humiliation and despair, the memory of which he could never shake off. Despite miserable circumstances and adversities, he could learn to read and write at night. Lesser mortals would have sunk in despair and disappeared in obscurity.

What catapulted him to the pinnacle of glory as an outstanding novelist of all times was sheer determination, solid will and an indomitable spirit to survive the "worst of times" and make it the "Best of Times." David Copperfield and Oliver Twist—the two priceless gifts Dickens gave to the world in fact epitomised the chill penury he had to endure during his formative years. He did realise his "Great Expectations just narrating" The tale of Two cities. He remains an inspiration for generations of budding writers.

A malnourished black boy, JESSE OWENS, son of a janitor in Cleaveland, Ohio, USA, caught the attention of a physical Education Teacher—a white-man, during the early part of the Twentieth century. The lanky lad would rush out of school during evenings to earn a few cents at a petrol bunk to support family income. His physical education teacher never minded paying Owens the cents earned in a part-time job because he knew the athletic potential of the young boy. Under his patronage and encouragement the young lad grew up to become the fastest human in the USA. The legendary athlete Jesse Owens rose to phenomenal heights and created four World records in Berlin Olympics in 1936 in 100 metres, 200 metres, Long Jump and 4 x 100 metres relay race! He could harvest four gold medals and thus bring name and fame to the country that brought his ancestors to the land of promise to sweat as labourers in cotton fields. Only two decades later another black-man, CARL LEWIS broke the records of his predecessor and rewrote history! Lewis worshipped Owens. Very few might be aware of the rigorous training Owens received for years at school under the watchful guidance of a white man, to become the fastest human locomotive by sheer perseverance and practice! It was not a cakewalk!

Poet LONGFELLOW once said

> "The heights by great men reached and kept
> were not attained by sudden flight;
> but they, while their companions slept,
> were toiling upward in the night."

Thomas Carlyle took several years to complete his "magnum opus"—FRENCH REVOLUTION. He gave the manuscript to his friend JOHN STUART MILL for comments. The blacket days of Carlyle began when Stuart Mill came to his study one morning and said:

"I don't know how to tell this but the manuscript you gave me, I read half of it and left at the mantelpiece. Well, the maid used it to start the fire." years of painstaking work were reduced to ashes in a second!

Carlyle was dumbfounded! He alternated between rage and grief. But he finally settled into deep despair. One day, he looked out of his window and saw bricklayers at work. It came to him that as they laid brick on brick, he could still lay word on word, sentence on "Sentence! With that he began to rewrite "French Revolution". The work he brought out endures to this day as a classic in its field and a monument to the kind of courage that alone can conquer despair!

An English Theologian once said:

> "Great occasions do not make heroes
> or cowards. They simply unveil
> them to the eyes of men. Silently
> and imperceptibly as we wake or
> sleep, we grow strong or weak
> and at last some crisis shows us
> for what we have become!"

"The reasonable man adapts himself to the world; the unreasonable one persists in trying to adapt the world to himself. Therefore all progress depends on the unreasonable man"

—*Bernard Shaw*

76

Some Thoughts on Mental Health

An unprecedented flood of literature has been unleashed on the subject of Mental Health in the latter half of the Twentieth Century. Caught in the whirlpool of worldly worries, agonies and anxieties on account of an accelerated pace of living and cut-throat competition in every sphere of human activity man desperately seeks relief and redressal. Some magazines provide instant remedy in the format of a few Do's and Dont's as though one could so easily gain everlasting bliss and tranquillity. The antidotes sound impressive and soothing as well. Some might suggest a few anachronistic religious austerities whereby the evil spirits could be exorcised and benign ones propitiated so as to remain sane. Sometimes their language would sound eerie and esoteric. The tribe of palmists seem to be on the increase and they dispense mental health for a price. One could be assured of a hundred percent success for a hundred-rupee-note. But the less privileged could also obtain a remedy for a fiver! It is very much akin to arresting a headache with a plain aspirin or a costly injection. Some would display an enlarged picture of palm on the pavement and diagnose all ills through a magnifying glass—the indispensable instrument for fortune forecast! The criss-cross lines on the palm seem to seal one's life, after all!

Some of these soothsayers seek the intervention of lovely little parrots. These birds are reared in captivity and trained to ferret out of a pile of folders just one with their beaks and faithfully deliver the same to the bearded, saffron-clothed "Swamiji!" He would open and reveal the picture of some God or goddess and read out a few incomprehensible couplets that would be intelligible only to the well-trained Swamiji. They usually set up their out-door clinics under a shady tree not too far from a thoroughfare so as to be accessible to a large number of pedestrians. Every one has some trouble or other. Otherwise these soothsayers would be in trouble in making a living!

It is time we honestly asked ourselves why we suffer from this mental unrest. How cold we tide over the turbulent waves of day-to-day life? Should we surrender ourselves to the supernatural forces or should we believe that man creates his own destiny? Except for the natural calamities that takes us unawares, much of the tragedies of life could be traced to the faulty style of living. One's parentage, schooling, community life and profession shape and determine one's enjoyment of life. All these are changeable and hence capable of promoting mental health.

Everyone has to have a clear-cut goal in life. Goal-less life can be linked to a rudderless boat that gets adrift instead of forging toward a destination. Goals should be realistic and capable of attainment. These are related to one's level of aspiration. Setting too high or too low a level of aspiration in an indication of inadequate self-concept. Goals should neither be beyond one's reach nor too close to one's grasp. In either case, an individual may not be adequately motivated. Motivation in the mainspring of mental health.

There are PROXIMATE GOALS as well as TRANSCENDENTAL GOALS. Proximate goals are immediate and closeby that can be attained within a shorter time-frame. Transcendental goals are remote ones that can be reached only through sustained effort stretched over a long period of time. A series of proximate goals lead to the ultimate goal, namely, SELF ACTUALISATION conceptualised by Abraham Maslow. It is the stage where one reaches PEAK EXPERIENCE. According to Allport this stage helps one to attain FUNCTIONAL AUTONOMY—a stage where one does not act merely to obtain a reward but autonomously. Carl Rogers considers such a person a FULLY FUNCTIONING individual—a kind of self-fulfilment born out of the fullest realisation of all that one is capable of. Teachers can assist a great deal in helping every individual set a goal in consonance with one's capacity.

Another ingredient of mental health is robust optimism in life "The optimist sees the rose and not its thorns; the pessimist stares at the thorn, oblivious of the rose" Observed Khalil Gibran. Life may not be an unending royal road of smooth surface to skate through. It has ups and downs. One may have to trudge and traverese through torrid terrain. However, as one marches ahead, one might come across a cool stream of limpid water, a cascade of waterfalls, to drench and quench one's parched lips, and vast green meadows to roll over or lie down, and resplendent rainbow providing a feast to vision. In other words, everyone has to face vicissitudes in life. Challenges in life strengthens one's Will and resolve to live amidst adversities. Mental health is related to the resilient frame of mind that facilitates adaptation.

In his famous essay, "Impact of Science on Society," Bertrand Russell writes:

> "Mankind is in the position of a man climbing a difficult and dangerous precipice at the summit of which there is a plateau of delicious mountain

> of meadows. With every step that he climbs, his fall, if at all he does fall, becomes more terrible, with every step his weariness increases and the ascent grows more difficult. At last, there is only one more step to be taken, but the climber does not know this because he cannot see beyond the jutting rocks at his head. His exhaustion is so complete that he wants nothing but rest. If he lets go, he will rest in death. HOPE Calls!" One more effort perhaps it will be the last effort indeed." IRONY retorts, "Silly fellow." Haven't you been listening to hope all this time and see where it has landed you." OPTIMISM says, "while there is life there is hope—PESSIMISM growls." While there is life there is pain." Does the exhausted climber make one more effort or does he let himself sink into the abyss? In a few years those of us who are still alive will know the answer."

Everyone dwells in two worlds — the world of FANTASY and REALITY. Both complement each other. The world of reality helps one to plan and live in the world of real persons and circumstances, accept personal limitation as well as situational constraints with complacency and humility. However, one cannot help occasional escape into the realm of imagination—a kind of make-believe world. Study of Literature, reading of poetry, listening to good music witnessing a classical dance or drama afford everyone a welcome diversion from the stress and strain of living. Life would have been insipid and intolerable bereft of these entertainments. These are harmless tranquillisers. However, one should not forsake reality and responsibility and seek refuge in the world of fantasy. Addiction to television—viewing not only spoils one's vision but one's mission in life. It shuts off socialisation and other healthy recreations.

Youngsters need to play vigorous games during evenings and cultivate a love for reading during nights. Schooling is not only to expand one's intellectual horizon but to circumscribe and crystalise one's aptitudes. Energy should not be dissipated but directed towards worthwhile pursuits. Creativity sprouts out of such endeavours.

What is the role of RELIGION in human affairs? It has become the stock-in-trade among the self-styled rationalists to pooh -pooh religion and prayer as though it is a kind of opium indulged in by the weak-minded. Belief in the existence of a FORCE far beyond the human force provided everyone with an anchorage when one gets tossed and assailed by worldly turmoil. A stress-free life is an utopia. In times of difficulty one needs something for support and succour. Psychotherapists look upon prayer as a kind of CATHARSIS by which one could purge off feelings of suffering and suffocation in the presence of a deity or by uttering devotional hymns with faith and fervour. Idol worship in not idle worship, but an ideal worship and if one feels better and lighter after unloading all troubles in the from of an worship why should we attempt a rational appraisal of an emotional experience! Perhaps this might help one to conquer the lower "self" so as to reach the higher SELF. The lower "self" is chained to passions while the exalted SELF in governed by reason and rectitude. One needs to remain "self-less" to realise one's SELF.

Envy and jealousy are the twin foes of mental health. Both are nurtured by feelings of inferiority and undue comparison with one's fellow human beings. Eventually this paves the way for self-condemnation and annihilation. Every creation of God is unique and endowed with some potentialities, that would blossom under adequate effort and environmental opportunities. If one were to fail to capitalise on his assets and dwell over imaginary or real liabilities one has to blame oneself. In the not-too-distant past, even a primary school teacher would maintain a robust self-image and pride, because he was aware that he was laying the foundation for a promising future among his students. He gave of his best and received reciprocal gratitude and respect. He remained contented playing the role of a ladder by which his students climb up in life. That kind of self-assurance, the dignity in class, the decency in community, that stoical acceptance of a life of spartan simplicity and humility seem to be totally extinct among the contemporary teaching community. An obsession to amass wealth by fair or foul means, triggered by a feeling of jealousy has driven most teachers to degrade and downgrade teaching from a profession to a tricky trade! It seems impossible to arrest this downward rend. It is bound to affect the mental health of teachers as well as students.

Our thoughts are shaped by what we feed into our minds. Discreet and discriminative reading is the "sine qua non" of good schooling Books and magazines of all kinds inundate the bookstalls and libraries. One has to be selective. One needs to be weaned from those that glorify vulgarity and portray obscenity with impunity. One has to move toward sublimity. To a considerable extent teachers instil in students a love of reading during the formative years that would sustain all through life. The seed of good taste sown in tender minds would germinate and take firm roots!

Fill your mind with fragrant thoughts and noble ideals. Do not make it a dumping ground to stuff with squalor. Let multicoloured flowers bloom, manicured lawns maintained, lush greenery and trimmed trees abound, slient stream flow, gushing waterfalls, descend, birds, bees and butterflies twitter that would please a Ruskin Bond or a Robert Frost. Retreat from the concrete jungle to a real jungle if you wish to preserve your mental health—

Postscript:

THE AMISH-SIMPLE FOLKS

In the state of Pennsylvania, USA, we find some simple folks—THE AMISH — who emigrated from switzerland in the early 1700s and who continue to live a typical Biblical "Plain Life." They live in Ohio, Indiana, and Pennsylvania. The magazine SPAN carried an article in the April issue of 1983 titled "THE WAY OF THE PLAIN FOLK." It is too plain to believe. Here are some excerpts:

> "The temperature is far below zero, and the morning dark and still. The kitchen is warm and glowing with the light of a kerosene lamp—The smell of fresh bread drifts through the house. Four-thirty in the morning does not come too early for the children of this farm family. Before breakfast, Elam and his son will tend their dairy hard. They will shovel out the manure pits and haul the manure away. Later they will spread it on the fields as fertilisers. All the work is done by hand. There are few machines and no electricity, telephone, on automobile on this farm."

77

Spreading the Light of Literacy

Historical events cannot be effaced. For nearly three centuries India was under colonial rule. The British used their imperialistic powers to subdue the country. Our forefathers were altruistic, righteous, though not literate. Most of them remained tillers and weavers. They remained complacent. All they needed was a roof to shield them from the sun and rain and some grains to stay alive. They were scattered all over the country, inhabiting thousands of hamlets and villages. India is a multilingual country. This proved to be a barrier to communication, unity and strength. Monarchy was in existence. Social inequality resulted in an unbridgeable gulf between the extravagantly rich and extremely impoverished populace. Frequent feuds among them strengthened alien rule. This absence of unity and solidarity among Indians was fully exploited by the British who used the "divide and rule" policy.

Education is the most powerful instrument of progress. Macaulay, the great intellectual of the British Kingdom devised a scheme of education of help administration. The cream of the Indian community could have access to higher education and also coveted positions in the Indian Civil Service. However, prestigious plum positions in the districts and states remained the prerogatives of the rulers. They needed an army of clerks and subordinate officers to fill in positions at lower levels. They needed a kind of education that would serve their needs. Macaulay fulfilled the aspirations of the rulers. Only a microscopic minority of Indians could have access to this elitist education. It never percolated to the mass of mankind living in far-flung hamlets. There was total apathy among the educated few to confer the benefit of literacy to the teeming illiterates. A kind of exploitation was prevalent. The wealthy landlords were happy that tillers and weavers remained illiterate.

Gandhiji who studied law in England and migrated to South Africa for legal practice was witness to the atrocities perpetrated by the arrogant British rulers upon the native blacks. He identified himself with the natives of South Afirca and many Indians who had migrated to that country. He had to undergo humiliation and incarceration. Lesser mortals would have buckled under the power of bayonet and baton. But Gandhiji was made of sterner stuff. He resorted to peaceful resistance or SATYAGRAHA, to fight for equal rights. The mighty British was humbled by a humble Indian by the humblest of weapons.

When Gandhiji returned to India, the country was still under British hegemony. It was in dire need of a crusader who could steer the people toward emancipation. Stalwarts like Gopalakrishna Gokhale, Balagangadhara Tilak were already in the forefront of the freedom struggle. Steel-hearted Vallabhai Patel, charismatic Jawaharlal Nehru, austere Acharya Kripalani and sagacious C. Rajagopalachari stood behind the leadership of Gandhiji. Strangely enough, Gandhiji visualised that only a pragmatic, indigenous system of education suited to the Indian ethos would transform Indian society. Even though he himself was a product of the British system of education, he had little faith in it. He conceived of a system known as Basic education that would be based on a craft. He had nothing but contempt for the glitter and glamour of Westernised education that made the educated more snobbish and alienated them from the masses. It was not an easy task. People who had been habituated to a pattern of education could not abandon it so easily and imbibe the philosophy of Basic Education.

Stated unambiguously, Basic education aimed at restoring the dignity of labor and productive work, is rooted to the immediate environmental needs, and also the holistic principle of knowledge. "Why should we segregate or compartmentalise disciplines at school?" Why shouldn't we unify, integrate, and make education more functional than ornamental, "wondered Gandhiji."

Perhaps his heart ached when he found cotton being confiscated and shipped to Lancashire U.K., to be sold in the Indian market as foreign clothes for fashionable folk! He wanted to universalise education so that it would reach every nook and corner of every village. What was the stark reality? Millions were illiterate. Can there be a more humiliating experience to an individual than affixing his thumb impression upon a stamped paper, the contents of which he would never know?

How many of these innocent villagers got cheated by the vain, wealthy landlords! Gandhiji realised the need for carrying the little lamp of Education to illumine every hut in every village. He realised the need for liberating masses for the shackles of ignornace and illiteracy alongside emancipation of his countrymen from the British rule.

Rural reconstruction was Gandhiji's major plank. He knew he was working against great odds. However, he was in the company of committed people. He never lost faith, never fumbled and never compromised. "Is it not better to light a candle than curse the darkness," thought Gandhiji.

He carried with him the lantern of hope, faith, and sincere prayer to achieve his goal. The world might have honoured him posthumously as the chief architect of India's freedom. Bapuji would have preferred to be remembered as someone who conceived and devised an educational system suited to the daily needs of people. In our euphoria and exuberance of ushering Information Technology, computer wizadry and a push button society, let us not forget the contribution of the immaculate Father of the Nation who strove hard all through his life to make every citizen literate!

The so-called illiterate villager may have an oceanic knowledge, and the much bloated city-bred citizens may have unfathomable ignorance of a few facts of life. A farmer is not a muff! He knows how to select the seeds and seedlings; how to sow; how much and how long he should water the field; how to dig canals; how to plough the land; how to harvest; how to store grains; how to sell it in the market and so on. He knows how to raise cattle, how to maintain poultry and so on. He may also have some elementary knowledge of herbal medicine to cure the common cold and fever. He has some knowledge of environmental hygiene. He does not need psychiatric assistance to cope with stress! On the negative side, he is rustic, unsophisticated, poorly dressed, has no knowledge of stocks and shares. He could easily be duped by clever literates. He cannot understand the meaning of secularism, communism and other jargons traded by politicians. We can say he is educated though illiterate! Just because a villager has not attended schools and colleges and has not acquired degrees and certificates he is not a nincompoop!

To say that a farmer has no knowledge is to reveal one's

bankruptcy of what knowledge means. Whoever ventures to participate in the National Literacy Mission should approach people with humility and honesty. They are not meeting aborigines in a dark continent or cannibals in Papua New Guinea. Rather they should join this National Movement with a missionary zeal so as to help their own countrymen!

In every town/district a voluntary organisation could be formed for the rural reconstruction. The scope of the National Literacy Mission should be broadened to include a comprehensive welfare-scheme. Perhaps, a retired person or a self-employed person could assume leadership. Identification of the village in close proximity should be the target. The team should visit the village and prepare a status report. It should include details like population, sex-wise, age-wise, number of dwelling, extent of land under cultivation, literates and illiterates, occupation of people etc. Volunteers from several walks of life should constitute the Task Force. Visits to villages could be during the week-ends or week-days, depending upon the convenience of members. The head of the village must be informed in advance so that the villagers cold assemble under the shade of a tree. The leader of the team could address the congregation about the need and importance of minimum literacy for a good life. They should be informed how a cooperative effort could transform village life into a vigorous, vibrant society. A holistic planning could be thought of, that should include knowledge of environmental health and hygiene, improved methods of cultivation, proper selection of manure and pesticide, storage of grain in warehouse, adequate fumigation to prevent decay, marketing of the produce, generation of power using gobar gas, poultry farming, carpentry, smithy and so on. The kind of education imparted to the illiterate villagers must be need-based and functional. An awareness for reconstruction must be created by the volunteers. Much depends on the motivation of the team members who join the mission.

A school in a city or town should have many classrooms, a laboratory, library, playground and adequate furniture in each classroom. But, in the National Literacy Mission, (NLM) we may not need such paraphernalia. With the help of the villagers a small hall could be constructed with thatched roof and mud-flooring to accommodate the rural folk in batches. All of them need not attend classes simultaneously. If an old temple premises is already available the place could be cleaned for use to conduct classes. Since the villagers are familiar with the spoken language the task of the literacy campaign would be made lighter. Instructional materials should be prepared in such a manner that the villagers would be motivated to learn. They do not compete for grades and ranks. Therefore, the tension of learning could be conspicuously absent. Social service organisation like the Rotary Club, Lion's club might provide a mobile van fitted with television to be shown to the villagers. Villagers would be delighted to watch programmes that have relevance to their day-to-day work. Eradication of evils such as drinking could be achieved by specially designed video-programmes. The women-folk are reformed. The volunteers should observe patience to get positive results. No attempt should be made to impart the city culture in the village and spoil the peace and tranquillity of rural atmosphere. Rather the villagers must be made to preserve their identity as a distinct entity. Both the volunteers and the villagers must experience a refreshing change for a better quality of life and living. There is no ready-made recipe or rule book to follow. What works in one village may or may not work in another village. When the villagers are taken as partners in progress they evince greater enthusiasm. It is a kind of education to the volunteers themselves, because they carry out programmes not found in textbooks, but evolved out of interaction.

Everyone is born healthy. But unhealthy surroundings

can cause diseases of several kinds. While the human metabolism restores normal health in course of time, some infectious diseases need proper treatment. All medical colleges have a department known as Social and Preventive Medicine. Faculty members take students in batches to nearby villages to conduct health camps. Several International organisations such as WHO and UNICEF provide funds to procure drugs for free distribution to patients undergoing treatment in a village health-clinic. As the villagers assemble to receive treatment for sickness at health centres they could be educated about small family norms, personal hygiene, proper balanced diet, and family planning. Incidental, non-formal modes of learning could be far more effective than formalised institutionalised learning. While medicines could be distributed free for minor ailments, serious cases should be shifted in an ambulance-van to the nearby hospitals in cities. Sound mind in a sound body is a familiar saying. Therefore, as part of the NLM, health and hygiene must receive priority.

It would not be out of place here to mention the miraculous transformation of sholiga tribals inhabiting B.R. Hills near Chamaraja Nagar in Karnataka. This writer was witness to the rehabilitation work when he took his students for a village camp life. The brain and brawn behind this transformation is Dr. Sudarshan, recipient of the Right Livelihood Prize —alternate Nobel Prize, from the Royal Swedish Academy last year! Twenty five years ago Mr. Sudarshan had to bear the agony of witnessing his father dying on his lap in a village bordering Andhra Pradesh and Karnataka. Since medical assistance was not easily available in the village, life of the old man could not be saved. At that juncture itself Mr. Sudarshan vowed to study medicine and work in a rural area.

Fortunately he could secure a seat in a medical college on merit. Soon after the completion of MBBS, Dr. Sudarshan went to Rishikesh on a short holiday. It was ordained that he should meet a Swamiji belonging to the Ramakrishna Mutt who advised him to go to B.R. Hills and work for the welfare of the tribals. nspired by the teachings of Sri Ramakrishna Paramahamsa and Swami Vivekananda, Dr. Sudarshan went up the B.R. Hills and started his rehabilitation programme. He set up a small clinic and would walk up the hilly region to the huts of the tribals with his medical kit to provide treatment. He chose to remain a bachelor. He wore coarse khadi clothes, lived in a small hut, slept on a mat upon the mud floor, ate simple ragi food along with the tribals and led a spartan life.

Dr. Sudarshan started a small primary school to educate the tribals. When the news spread several volunteers joined his mission to offer free service. He would be present at the morning Assembly, pray and sing the National Anthem along with children. He restored the dignity and self-respect of the poor tribals. He set up a small cottage industry to make agarbathis. Several International voluntary organisations donated medicine, equipment, ambulance van and also monetary fund to build his project. Dr. Sudarshan donated the entire prize-amount he received from the Royal Swedish Academy to the B.R. Hills Project. He fought with the Local Government the right of ownership of the land that the tribals cultivated. People, young and old, look upto the middle aged bachelor-doctor with love and regard.

How do we treat our less fortunate human beings. Most of us pity them, some sympathise, a few lend a helping hand, majority mind their business. Years ago, when Anne Sullivan, HELEN KELLER'S teacher first met her pupil, she found a six-year old, who was blind, deaf and as uncontrollable as a wild animal. The child tyrannised her family. If she did not get her own way she would pinch, kick or bite!

Was Anne Sullivan contemptuous toward that poor creature? Did she write her off? Anne Sullivan was concerned. She cared for that young girl, not realising that the girl one day, would stun humanity by an indomitable will! Every time the little girl Helen pinched her she gave a mild slap. Cruelty! No. Attention? Yes, attention backed by affection, motivated by concern. Later, when Helen Keller wrote her memoirs, the slaps were forgotten as she recalled that day when she met her beloved teacher for the first time.

> "I felt the approaching footsteps.
> I stretched out my hand as I
> supposed, to my mother. Someone
> took it and I was caught up
> and held close in the arms of her
> who had come to reveal all things
> to me, and, more than all things
> else, to love me."

ACTION PLAN

(i) Do not collect more than a dozen or a maximum of twenty for conducting class so that interaction is possible and feasible.

(ii) Teach them a prayer and also the National Anthem. Explain the meaning so that their National pride could be aroused and awakened.

(iii) Teach them letters of the alphabet in their mother-tongue. Train them to sign their name. Give practice. Let them not use their thumb-impression any more.

(iv) Read out the headlines from a newspaper. Let them come to know who really care for them and serve them. Let them also know who are self-seekers and opportunists!

(v) Educate them on how valuable their votes are. Let them not be taken for a ride by professional politicians.

(vi) Narrate instances from the Epics like *Ramayana, Mahabharatha* so that they can know the ultimate triumph of truth over falsehood.

(vii) Teach them some folk songs and let them enjoy singing together.

(viii) Attempt to restore their dignity and self-respect. After all they belong to our country.

(ix) Do not give a hint that all that you do is charity. It is your duty and a pleasant duty at that!

"I don't need a friend who changes when I change and who nods when I nod; my shadow does that better"

— *Plutarch.*

"Life's journey is along an uncharted path where hills and hollows overtake us unawares"

—*Tagore.*

78

Coping with a Crisis

Life will be pretty smooth-sailing if everything works out to our plan and design. Does it always happen? What will you do if you are taken unawares? Do you cry? Do you collapse? The situation that is overwhelming and demoralising is called a CRISIS. The term "crisis-management" is in current usage. It calls for something more than intelligence. We may call it `flexibility'! A more appropriate term is 'resiliency'. We extol those who display such a trait. Is it a superhuman ability, reserved for the extraordinary? It is partly true, perhaps. One can always gain by others' experience. Here is one such instance.

One day John Stuart Mill entered the study-room of Thomas Carlyle with a sullen face. He was rather hesitant to open the subject. "I don't know how to tell you this, my friend," began Stuart Mill and continued. "The manuscript you gave me to read—well, the maid used it to start fire." (The manuscript was Carlyle's `magnum opus' THE FRENCH REVOLUTION!)

Carlyle listened calmly, though he was quite upset. Rage and grief gripped him alternately. Ultimately, Carlyle settled into despair. There was no use crying over spilt milk. He was looking through the window at some brick-layers placing brick upon brick to erect a wall. Carlyle thought, "Why shouldn't I do the same thing—Lay word upon word, sentence upon sentence? Thus began his classic—THE FRENCH REVOLUTION. This work spurred CHARLES DICKENS to bring out another classic—"A TALE OF TWO CITIES"!

One should not recoil under the crisis. A crisis is a challenge. One should learn to welcome and cope with it. Do you know, most writers faced acute disappointments in their early attempts. Manuscripts would be rejected. Unpublished, rejected ones always outnumber the published ones. They do not get disheartened. They persevere. Becoming a good writer is a painfully slow process. It is like a bud blossoming into a flower. There is one difference. A bud turns into a flower overnight. But, one does not become a writer overnight, but over several nights and days! Let me recount one experience of mine.

I was invited for a seminar. I worked on the subject allotted to me earnestly and did considerable library work for two weeks. I preserved the material in a file carefully. I was at the venue on the scheduled date and time. I was expectant and quite excited. The chairman introduced me to the gathering. All eyes were on me. I opened my brief case and was in for a shock! The file was missing. My heart skipped a beat. I realised I had brought the wrong file. Ironically, the subject on which I was to speak was "Coping with a crisis." I never expected that I would have to really cope with a crisis. I did it!

I faced the audience and started speaking extempore. I narrated anecdote after anecdote from memory. I could perceive the effect upon the audience. They listened. I do not know how I managed. Toward the end I disclosed how I had to really cope with a crisis! I received a standing ovation! I could not have done better even with my prepared script.

In times of crisis, your real potentiality surfaces and saves you.

One does not know how such crisis would hone your skill and shape your personality. One should not slacken effort on that score. Carlyle could rewrite his book because his earlier labour stood him in good stead. Perhaps, his second version might have been an improvement. Who knows? Because, the earlier work was 'utilised' by the maid to start the fire! Did it fire the enthusiasm of Carlyle to begin once again with redoubled effort? He had to cope with a crisis, anyway.

> "Democracy is always a beckoning goal, not a safe harbour. For freedom is an unremitting endeavour and never a final achievement"
>
> — *N.A. Palkhivala.*

79

Remembering the Past, Reflecting on the Future, Dwelling in the Present

A good many of us have a tendency to anticipate pain in the future like: "What will happen to my family if I die of heart attack?" "Will my business collapse in this competitive world?" "Will I deliver my speech well next week in the inaugural function of the college union?" "Will I complete my studies creditably?" The list is endless!

Quite a number feel depressed, guilty and sorrowful over their commissions and omissions of the past. They brood, brood and brood all the time. I shouldn't have changed my job!;" "I shouldn't have chosen this course!" "I shouldn't have married! "I shouldn't have gone abroad." We can fill the whole page listing such endless regrets.

We have a microscopic minority, firmly rooted to the present—neither lamenting over the bitter past nor building castles in the air far a rosy future! We may call them pragmatists.

"Living in the moment means being aware of your power in the present." says JEFF DAVIDSON.

Those who choose to dwell in the past would recall their golden days when this good earth was less populated, less polluted, education less expensive but more exemplary, ethics, less professed but more practised. Such people lack resiliency to adapt themselves to the changing ways of living.

Those die-hard pessimists who would fail to enjoy the sight of a rose but only, stare at the thorns would recall vividly and kaleidoscopically the blunders and bad times of the unpleasant past. They indulge in self-pity!

Dreamers are of two kinds. Those who can translate their dreams into reality, and those who translate reality into a dreamy state! Great scientists and social reformers belong to the first category. All shirkers and "good-for-nothing" type would merely dream but do practically nothing to make it happen. Some are prone to nightmarish dreams, imagining that the high-rise building might crumble down like the World Trade Center, New York. They would always be on the look-out for bleak prospects!

We are left with very few who live only in the present. They have their daily routine. Gardeners, construction workers, Teachers and Doctors live more for others than for themselves. Let us follow their footsteps to make life worth living!

80

Humour in the Classroom

Traditionally we have grown accustomed to consider Schooling and Education as a serious business. A kind of solemnity or austerity is associated with the personality of a teacher whose single-minded duty is to inform, inculcate, instil knowledge and wisdom to pupils. The preceptor is expected to be goal-directed,time-conscious and result-oriented. Digression is discouraged and idleness is prohibited. Sounds nice of course! Perhaps R.K. Narayan and his dear brother R.K. Laxman too must have gone through this suffocation in their classes amidst grim-placed hard task-masters. With a vengeance the elder brother took to caricature through writing satirical short stories and novels and the younger brother took to cartooning to expose the hollowness of high profile political heavy-weights! Evidently, they must have pursued these prohibited pastimes surreptitiously. Otherwise, short-tempered teachers would have given them a dressing down in the open class or expelled them from the school! Nevertheless both the brothers became celebrities and the whole world adore them! We do not know whether their class-fellows, loyal, obedient, achievement-obsessed, bright bookworms caught the public attention or remained in oblivion. They might have been the favourites of dedicated teachers. Does humour have a place in the classroom? The answer is 'Yes'. Not that, I mean buffoonery or clownish behaviour. Teachers have to have a sense of humour.

Humour is like a whiff of perfumery. It pervades fast, relieves boredom and monotony and compels attentiveness. Often a teacher can convey an idea better by spicing it with a little bit of fun. Here is an illustration. Handwriting is a skill that is imparted meticulously in primary classes. Teachers are harsh on those who write shabbily and illegibly. Children are mercilessly goaded to do transcription exercises to improve their handwriting. It is not advisable to emulate Mahatma Gandhi in this respect as we all know his handwriting was not that good. Legibility is the main criterion. Some eminent doctors prescribe medicines that can be deciphered only by the chemists is drug stores. Good handwriting is an asset and can often compensate for diction. How should a teacher deal with a student whose handwriting is atrocious? Here is the remark:

> "Your handwriting looks as if a swarm of ants, escaping from an ink-bottle had walked over a sheet of paper without wiping their legs."

The whole class would have a good laugh including the student who was targetted! Does not it require creativity to make such an observation?

Everyone knows that the last hour in the time-table is really a lost hour, an unwelcome period to teach any subject. Because, most of the students would be awaiting the last bell to disperse. Some teacher has to be a sacrificial goat! Here is a teacher who invented a story to keep the class in good humour. Usually Sardarji jokes are popular (though not in Punjab!) One Sardarji was travelling by Tamilnad Express from Chennai to New Delhi and he was allotted the last compartment. The blessed train had only a few stops. Wherever it halted, the last compartment was way beyond the platform. Hence the Sardarji missed all the fun of vendor of sweets and samosas, fruits and biscuits and what not!

He lost the fun of watching varied brands of passengers and hawkers. He could see only the gravel and goods shed! By the time the train reached New Delhi Railway Station the Sardarji was fretting and fuming and hissing like a cobra! "Come on, where is the complaint book," thundered the well-built soldier!" He made only two comments:

(i) There should be no last compartment to a train.

(ii) Should there be one, it should be somewhere in the middle! Similarly there should be no last period in the school time-table. Should there be one it should be somewhere in the middle!"

The class burst into boisterous peals of laughter. I cannot, however, forget a young girl of nineteen, a teacher trainee handling an English Class in the last period, enlisting the undivided attention of everyone in the class. She was really a gifted teacher indeed!

The first period in the afternoon session is equally a detestable one. Students cannot help dozing after a good lunch. It requires enormous effort to keep the eyelids open. Finding most of his students dozing during his afternoon lecture, the Pathology Professor thumped on the table and burst out: "there is a controversy as to which is the real moment of death—When the brain ceases to work or when the heart stops functioning. I do not know which is correct, but if it is the former, then I am compelled to pronounce most of this class as dead!" Everyone woke up to listen to the meaning and definition of death!

One day, in the Political Science class the Professor and a student became engaged in a heated discussion, which grew more and more involved as it progressed. The student suddenly realising that the Professor had shifted his position said rather confidently. "But, sir now you're arguing my side of the question." "I know" responded the Professor. "Your side wasn't doing too well."

Bernard Shaw is well-known for his slicing humour. He always has the last word: He said: "England and America are to countries separated by the same language!"

Mark Twain observed: "I never let schooling interfere with my education."

Humorous anecdotes during a lesson can enliven the class a great deal. It is not a sin to smile or laugh in the classroom. However, a teacher should not become a joker!

> "The only way to get rid of temptation is to yield to it".
>
> —*Oscar Wilde*

81

The TV Toll

Just about a couple of decades ago when the electronic media made inroads into our drawing room we were in the Seventh Heaven. By pressing a button we could have before us lands we had never visited or might never visit at all. Zoom lens made it possible to watch Boris Becker cursing, spitting venom when his forehand smashed the net rather than the court beyond. We could also perceive the subtle movements of eye-brows, frowns upon forehead, widening of the pupils of the eyes of a 'kathakali dancer from Kalamandalam, Kerala. It looked as though the News reader was reading just for us and us alone! However, we had to put up with the sub-standard skits in languages that we never followed and also melodrama that we had stopped appreciating long ago! Of course there was a rich haul of twists, dances, dives, somersaults and a merry-go-round of our favourite-film-stars to the accompaniment of cacophony, called music. We also had the spiderman performing incredible feats, skating in the air from New York Empire State Building to some other tower to save a lady from the clutches of a ruffian and goblin! No doubt we had good entertainment. But, it had its toll too!

Drawing-room chat with friends, and family members had been given a farewell. In fact very few call on us during "Prime Time," or we do so lest it might come in the way of watching the favourite 'masala' movies! Even if someone were to venture to drop in, he would be shown his place—a vacant chair—to sit and watch the small screen silently and keep his mouth shut! He will have to leave graciously if he does not like the Idiot box.

Reading time of newspapers has been drastically cut, particularly on Sunday when we have almost non-stop shows in quick succession. Intermittent advertisements for soaps, sandals, sweets, saris, scented sticks shaving creams, supari and what not can generate sickness or seething anger because these cut into the sequence of a masala movie!

You glance at the headlines of the newspaper and also the Sunday Supplement running to about forty pages and hope to read it at leisure. Where is the leisure so long you have the little devil in the drawing room drawing your attention! You reconcile yourself to the inevitable though mentally you might be dwelling upon something else.

If only the Almighty had not blessed us with the power of imagination to withdraw ourselves from our drawing room we would have been choked to death!

By 8.30 at night you are ready for supper as you are sufficiently famished. Soon after, you get a little respite to read the newspaper that you abandoned in the morning, to catch up with the news—National and Multinational as well as the magazine section, only to be hooked once again to the small screen. The smart-looking newsreader would brief you with the latest goings-on -the decisions and indecisions, the discretions and the indiscretions, the genocide in some parts of the world — when the newspaper is once again sidelined!

Your eyelids droop down inviting you to bed to lull you to sleep and call it a day! The following day the newspaper is collected, arranged and shelved. All your favourite novels gather dust on the bookshelf and remains show-pieces to give a false impression to the visitors that you are a voracious reader!

82

Far From the Madding Crowd

Once upon a time there lived a boy in a village. It was far, but not too far, from a town. Most people in that village were farmers. Some owned lands while some cultivated others lands. A bus used to pass by the main road once in the morning and another time in the evening. Hardly anyone would get down or board it. Hence, it would rarely halt. The boy used to squat on a big stone under a greenwood tree near the river-bed and watch the bus inquisitively. Lots of dust would be raised because the road was not tarred. During rainy days cesspools of water would get collected and this would be sprayed whenever the bus would pass. No one would be around to be drenched by the muddy water.

The boy nursed a desire to board the bus some day and go to town. He had never gone out of the village since birth and he was just ten years old. His father did not own any land. He was a poor farmer. His mother would make cow-dung cakes all through the day while his father would leave home in the early hours and return only at dusk. The boy would take the cow and buffalo to the fields adjoining the river for grazing. He would sit under the green-wood tree and sing some folk songs. He wasn't a good singer at all. But, he enjoyed singing. When he would feel hungry he would return home to eat whatever was available. His mother would serve what little she had with lots of love and care. Pretty soon he would be back to his work spot.

One day he found a visitor at home. He saw him getting down from the bus. But he did not know that he was a distant relative from the nearby town. He was working in some factory. Mother introduced the boy to the uncle. The uncle was pleased and asked whether he could take the boy to town along with him. Mother could not take a decision. But her son was eager to go to town in a bus. His father was sent for. Reluctantly the parents consented to send the boy. He was jumping with joy. He put on his crumpled shirt and packed his clothes in a small bag and was ready in a trice. However, he was to leave only in the evening because the bus was not frequently plying. As he boarded the bus with the uncle his father and mother saw him off with glistening eyes. But he was excited and occupied a window seat close to the driver's seat. He liked the noise of the engine as it accelerated and the gears were changed. Looking through the window he counted the trees and canals and surveyed the fields stretching and meeting the horizon far far away. After an hour the bus reached the turn. The boy could see many houses and shops, cyclists, bullock-carts, and several people. Everyone seemed to be busy. The boy acompanied the uncle to his house. It was a small house among a row of houses. However, it was certainly more tidy than his hut in the village. There were a few chairs, a bench, a cycle, an almirah and plenty of vessels. He was introduced to a fat lady, perhaps wife of the uncle. She surveyed him head to foot and sternly ordered to keep his bag in a corner. From their conversation in the adjoining room the boy could gather that she needed a girl than a boy for help. Perhaps they had no children. The uncle pleaded with her that the boy was good enough. Anyway, the boy felt rather displeased at their unwelcome gesture. But, he was too poor to be sensitive. He remained silent.

The boy had to sweep the house, water the plants in the garden, collect water from the tap, run errands to procure vegetables and grocery. He had never done all these things in his village. One day he was reprimanded for bringing things from the shop not listed. It was not his fault, anyway. The shop-keeper messed it up. But the boy did not know how to argue. Gradually he came to realise that he had no freedom to do what he wanted and go out as he liked. He felt he was rather imprisoned. He craved to get back home. He did not find the food prepared by the aunt tasty. He longed to eat food prepared by his dear mother. He fell ill one-day. He was sleeping longer than usual. He was awakened by the aunt and asked to attend to work. He started sobbing and complained of headache and weakness. The aunt wanted to get rid of the boy somehow. He asked her husband to take the boy to village and leave him with his parents and get a girl instead.

The day of departure thrilled him beyond expression. Even at that time the aunt was pretty stern and stiff. However, the boy was so happy to leave for his village. All along the bus-travel he was thinking of his mother, cows, buffalo and the greenwood tree underneath which he had spent countless hours. The journey seemed longer as he was pretty anxious to reach home. At last the bus reached the village limits and the conductor blew the whistle. The boy and the uncle got down. The boy ran home and fell into the arms of his mother. Both of them cried for a while. She hugged him and kissed him several times and gave him some sweets she prepared the previous day. The uncle took leave of them after offering some money to the lady. She valued her son more than the money she received. The boy ran to the backyard, patted his cow and buffalo and was soon off to the river-bed. Sitting under the greenwood tree he realised that sweet home is always sweet. He was happy to be far from the madding crowd of town life.

—

83

To Learn to Live Together

We are born alone; but we do not live all alone, because loneliness is not something pleasant to normal human beings. As we grow we recognise the need to be interdependent. Out of such cohesiveness emerges values, culture, civilisation, religion and humanism. Way back in the early part of this century we had more villages than towns and cities. People lived in harmony and peace in hamlets. Caste conflicts or the invidious divide of the 'haves' and 'have nots' were not witnessed. Seldom we came across instances of caste conflict that resulted in loss of life and property. Each one in a village knew each other and this comraderie helped a great deal to bring about rural development and welfare. Without fanfare and publicity and bulging bureaucracy people did voluntarily come forward to establish a closely knit community-life. There was an over-all prosperity despite a certain amount hierarchy. No one disrupted this order. It was found in every family. The eldest commanded respect and enforced a sense of discipline but did not pepetuate an authoritarian regime. There were occasions for mutual consultation and also instances for unilateral decisions, but the guiding spirit was always the preservation of the dignity of the individual. Since we were living together naturally we never had to learn to live together. We seem to be at the cross-roads now! We have forgotten how to live together. We need to draw some lessons from our own ancestors and sedulously cultivate a few traits that would unite than divide us.

During the thirties and forties we had a common enemy to fight namely the alien rule and a passion for emancipation. We felt that liberation from foreign domination would transform our life. We got united and fought a relentless war of "Satyagraha" under the stewardship of the Father of the Nation. We achieved freedom at midnight. At last the rulers left us to guide ourselves to evolve a government of people's representatives so as to usher in a Welfare State. Within a short span of half-a-century from the red-letter day we have come to realise how short-lived our pious expectations turned out to be! Villages have been deserted or desecrated. Unions sprang up to bring about disunity. Human needs gave way to greediness, sublimity to shoddiness and bonds to breaks and cleavages. Instead of resorting to mutual accommodation to settle minor differences we have provided accommodation for a jury to hear our petitions and thus perpetuate hostility and bitterness. We had a much smaller police force to maintain law and order since most of us had a policing force within ourselves in the form of conscience. We were perhaps naive to watch and enjoy movies that glorified virtue, benevolence, rectitude and harmony. Very few portrayed violence, vulgarity, vengeance and voluptuousness. We never had a hang-over when we left the theatres. Rather the good episodes lingered in our memory for days and weeks. We felt that as human beings we should learn to disagree aggreeably and learn to live together rather than wrecking human bonds and solidarity. We never even were familiar with the term `National Integration' because we never had disintegration. Perhaps this ethos of our country must have prompted (late) Humayun Kabir to write a book titled 'Unity in Diversity.'

It is time we resurrected some of the pristine glories and values that characterised humanity in the past and save the country from an imminent catastrophe. We need to usher in a Social order wherein we would live in peace, traders would not cheat customers by adulteration of food items, public servants would serve the public than expecting the public to serve them, needs would not be substituted by neediness and more opportunities to experience ecstasy rather than agony. It does not require a heavy outlay from the Finance Ministry or the International Monetary Fund loan to make this land where milk and honey would flow. All that it requires is the Will to respect the Divine Will and realise the Divinity embedded in every individual. We dig borewells to get water to quench our thirst. When are we going to dig wells in human hearts to get the fountain of love, sympathy and solidarity!

To quote RADHA NARAYAN of Canada:

A LEGACY LOST
We are given a legacy, a heritage
And now, engrossed in selfish cares
What have we done with it?
The numerous souls of India's past
Would probably look down, hearts bleeding
At the impoverished state of affairs
And think — was it all a waste!
We the people of India
Struggled as one for years
Towards Independence
And with blood, toil and tears,
We men, women and children
Won Swaraj - in 1947
And now, with sorrow I come to realise

That, in spite of a united legacy
We live our lives divided
In spite of an honest legacy
We live our lives corrupted
In spite of fighting for an independent legacy
The chains that once bound human kind
Have now bound the human mind.

84

Good Morning Friends and Good Friends!

Friendliness, I guess, is a human trait. We are not sure whether it is found among the subhuman species! We might find a flock of birds, herd of elephants, bevy of ants. Do these really interact the way human beings do? These birds and animals seem to be self-reliant and quite reticent. Do they have thought-processes? Anyway, devoid of the power of speech, these creatures are freed from heated argument over trivial issues. There is absolutely no scope for clash of views or ego inflation. You notice a kind of tranquillity among cows and buffaloes, when they graze silently upon the grass fields and chew the cud leisurely. They cast a benign look. While the "homo sapiens are feverishly seeking recourse to special yogic exercises to have STHITHAPRAJNA, these creatures pursue these paths without any tutors!

As a septuagenarian I have been witnessing a sea-change in human interaction particularly in big cities. Every one minds his business and they seem to have little time to stand and stare unlike the celebrated poet William Wordsworth, who watched silently, a solitary reaper and composed a sonnet! Viewed from a tall building human beings in big cities look like bees or ants, moving around, with their own sorrows and anxieties. Seldom do they seem to interact, to cry over the shoulders of friends and unburden their feelings of isolation and alienation! What a life, my God, in this Space Age that has created more space among living human beings, unlike their predecessors who lived in smaller towns and villages. I reminisce over the golden past when I make annual visits to my ancestral village far from the madding crowd, with only a few dotted houses amidst green friends and a few modest streams or rivers to bathe and wash. Such visits would give me everlasting bliss and peace that people yearn to get through soap opera and electronic media in cities!

The screeching sounds of sparrows and crows, acompanied by the cows in the backyard would wake up my aged grandmother, to brush her teeth, go to the cowshed, to have the first "darshan" of her pet cow "Gowri" as the illiterate lady had the pious belief that it is an auspicious thing to do to commence a day! Cows rest, but seldom sleep long hours as we do. They generously offer us milk, ungrudgingly and unfailingly every day. My granny would milk the cow and even talk to her a few endearing words. Cows are her trustworthy friends, I guess! Are not animals more honest and trustworthy?

Back to my city life. I reconcile myself to a life of anonymity and impersonality. The more a city grows the greater the alienation. The neighbourhood concept is almost extinct when they began to live in multistoreyed apartments unlike their ancestors who lived in small houses or huts in rural settings. We have a number of "Good morning friends" whom we greet everyday as a kind of custom or convention. Youngsters greet each other by some such sounds like "Hi" or "Hallo" and move on like an escalator in a departmental store!

During my morning walks to collect flowers for daily

pooja I greet a few familiar faces with my habitual "Namaskar" than "Good Morning," which again is replaced by Good Day"! Everyone seems to be in a hurry to complete the brisk walks sweating and panting like a marathon runner! Some would be holding the chain tied to a hideous-looking dog, preventing everyone from reaching its master. So you just smile and greet without words! Sometimes you wish a friend but it is not reciprocated. You feel bad. The other person might not intend to hurt or insult you, but might be preoccupied with some family problem. "Good morning" greetings seem to have lost the meaning because these have almost become reflex actions.

What do you do in an emergency? Someone is ill at home. You desperately need friendly help, which may not be available in the colony you live. You dial a number, and in a few minutes a friend arrives. He might be living in a different locality. But he is a trusted friend with whom you can open up your heart. He lends a helping hand. He is not a "Good Morning" friend, but a "Good friend."

A friend in need is a friend indeed!

85

Togetherness is No More

The craving for companionship, group-living, sharing and caring—are all traits that distinguish a well-knit community from an exploitative society or cut-throat competition. The tendency to alienate oneself and abjure socialisation can make human beings mere "bishops, rocks, horses and pawns" on a chess board, to be castled or checkmated!

"Leave me alone" is the usual refrain with many people of modern times. "Keep your problems to yourself. I have enough and to spare," is the cold rebuff one receives when one looks for someone on whom to unload the trials and tribulations of life.

Why is this so? Why have people chosen to be less humane? Is it the price that one has to pay for the mind-boggling style of life in most metropolitan cities? If one is not strong willed, capable of pulling one's own weight, one finds life, miserable in a depersonalised society.

Life was certainly more relaxed, warmer, more intimate in bygone days! Half a century ago our countrymen rejoiced and celebrated the liberation from colonial rule. I have lived in British India as well as Indian India! We had more homes than houses in those days! Every home had a granny. The grand old lady would have abdicated her powers to the rest of the younger generation so that she could live in peace for the rest of her life.

She would be busy in her own way —counting beads, reading classics like Ramayana, Mahabharataa, narrating endless tales of yore to little children, to put them to sleep pacify sobbing kids who had incurred the wrath of their overworked mothers and fathers. Yes, grannies were always indulgent, permissive and generous. That is why children stayed together and gathered around their grandmothers!

Alas! There is a shortage of such grannies these days. She is considered a nuisance, a burden, someone who is always ill. Her psychological health has suffered more than her physical health. She is discarded very much like a disposable syringe. She has to fend for herself. Children are dissuaded from getting close to her as she might spoil the youth by telling them fairy tales.

These days children are being brainwashed or stormed by super-computers, pagers, the internet and what not!

Discarded by everyone in the family, the grandmother has just to crouch in a corner while looking forward expectantly to her final destination!

86

Higher Education in Doldrums!

Education is the key to progress and prosperity. Investment in quality-education will never go waste. It is bound to pay dividends in the long run. The sooner we realised this truth, the better. Paradoxically, quality and quantity are inversely proportional. Quantitative expansion would be detrimental to the standard of education. Democracy or democratisation might be a laudable slogan in politics. Would it be valid in the sphere of education? We are witnessing today an incredible proliferation of colleges, particularly in professional courses such as Engineering and Medicine. We can not say that this movement is based on altruistic motives.

Financing higher education is becoming harder and harder. Once upon a time, Government was the sole Agency to promote such professional education. The coffers of the Government are almost empty. Hence all these institutions have to be self-supportive without getting grants from the government. Privatisation is unavoidable. They are left with no choice but to compel the students to bear the burden. Such institutions collect hefty fees plus donation for admission. So long this is done without sacrificing merit there will be no harm. But, this remains only a pipe-dram! The really deserving students have no wherewithal while the really undeserving ones have enormous resources to purchase seats! Quite unwittingly the promoters of self-financing colleges offer admission for a price. Money would keep pouring in. But, standards would be sliding down uncontrollably.

Are we not precipitating a social catastrophe. A kind of volcano would be in the making and the gestation period might be a couple of decades. When the output of trained engineers and doctors remain unchecked, society is bound to pay a heavy cost eventually. The merit of a degree issued from these citadels of learning would not even be worth the paper in which it is printed in the absence of a quality-control. Who is to blame for his social upheaval?

Financing higher education is the real issue. The unchecked growth of population necessitated unlimited expansion of educational opportunities. More and more institutions are opened to cater to the needs of the populace. The government is compelled to yield to the requests of private agencies to promote higher education. We witness today the sad spectacle of higher education in doldrums!

How do these institutions run the show? There is an acute shortage of really committed faculty to impart quality education in Medicine and Engineering. Meritorious graduates find the practice of medicine and Engineering much more lucrative and challenging than teaching in classrooms. Private clinics and nursing homes are mush-rooming in every nook and corner and the cost of health-care is beyond the reach of the middle-income group.

In Engineering there is a kind of hierarchy of specialisation. Information Technology graduates are offered mind-boggling pay and perquisities in private companies. Naturally, Engineering colleges are unable to attract the bright for teaching IT courses. Most of the students have more or less, reconciled to receive minimal assistance in classroom. They have to fend for themselves. While the bright can somehow manage, the not-so-bright-ones are left high and dry. Quality deterioration cannot be arrested under such circumstances. Do we have a solution for the mess we have created?

We need to take a few hard decisions:

— Declare a moratorium on the opening of medical and Engineering colleges for the next twenty-five years.

— Ruthlessly derecognise those existing colleges that do not maintain proper infrastructure and adequately qualified faculty.

— Ban outrageous donations collected by those private managements who run the show more as a commercial enterprise that as an educational institution.

— Raise the salary of the teaching faculty so as to attract bright members.

— Closely monitor classroom teaching so as to discourage shirking of responsibilities by the faculty.

— Deny admission to candidates below a cut-off point and never allow exceptions.

— Also educate parents not to brainwash their sons and daughters that a career in Engineering or Medicine alone could lead to prosperity.

87

Your Attention Please!

If you are at tension you cannot bestow attention. However, if you are too relaxed, it might result in laxity. You need to fine-tune yourself to absorb as much as you can from a lecture and avoid as best as you can the distracting stimuli. We have to fight from within as well as from those that lie in the external environment. The former pertains to our ever-changing moods, interests and also boredom and fatigue. Whenever you attend a lecture ensure you are free from undue anxiety or enormous expectation. Do not judge a speaker too hurriedly and curse yourself being in the hall. Just as a bus or a locomotive has a slow start, gradual acceleration to gain momentum so as to reach an optimum speed whereby passengers could feel safe and secure, a speaker also tends to spend a little time to attain his smooth flow of ideas. Unless the subject interests your concern, your occupation and appeals to your personal philosophy of life, you should not torture yourself by stepping into the meeting hall. It is not proper to disturb those who have gathered to listen and benefit from the talk. If you feel tired and exhausted due to inadequate sleep at night or a work-out session in a gym, better you stay away. You just cannot arrest the drooping eyelids, preceded by yawning.

Here are a few tips to the speaker to hold the attention of the audience. Plan in advance, jot down the key-points as well as the anecdotes appropriate to the subject of the lecture, proceed methodically keeping an eye on the eyes of the audience to get their silent feed-back. However, do not get over-excited by visible gestures. Sometimes it may be misleading! Reinforce the important messages by drawing their attention and changing the phraseology. A novice needs to rehearse well before ascending the platform. It is not prudent to be overconfident nor is it advisable to use too bombastic a language that would keep the listeners wondering. This simpler the presentation, the better. Make it short and sweet so that the audience do not start murmuring or get fidgety. Invite questions at the end, answer if you can, admit ignorance if you are not sure and say a word or two to thank them for being present. Do not overdo this as though you had never had a similar opportunity earlier. Nor should you say "thank you for your patient heaving" unless you encountered impatient hearing. Reflect back for the necessary correction.

88

Fair-Sex in the Fore Front

Kudos to the members of the fair-sex for their sterling performance in SSLC, PUC and CBSE Examinations! The days are not far off when they would outsmart their counterparts and capture top positions in the IAS and IFS too! Results of most examinations have catapulted the fair-sex to the fore-front! Assuming that there is no gender inequality with respect to Intelligence, how could these little angels steal a march over the boys? This is a subject that deserves careful attention by parents and educators. Notwithstanding exceptional cases wherein boys have asserted themselves, the percentage of passes clearly demonstrates the supremacy of girls. As a teacher of psychology for nearly four decades in colleges of Education, the author shares his perceptions.

One of the essential attributes of an ideal student is to bestow undivided attention to classroom teaching besides being punctual to the class. In this respect girls, by and large, score a point. They tend to be more systematic, studious and submissive. They never fail to submit assignments on time. They are quite conscientious, pretty sensitive, even hypersensitive, to their grades in examinations. They put in long hours of sustained study in their hostels or homes all through the year. They never pile up arrears of work to the last-minute preparation. They are less distracted by non-academic pursuits. Very few among girls in school join student-activism. Of course, you do find, here and there, a few tomboys in metropolitan cities indulging in activism! They are far too few in number-perhaps their scholastic performance may be poor. To compensate their lacklustre performance in class, they might have taken to such populist activities!

It would be unfair to downgrade boys wholesale. Not all people fall a prey to non-academic pursuits, which deflect their attention from scholastic work. However, do not boys, by and large, in most homes, enjoy greater freedom and privilege to do what they want to do, go wherever they decide to go? Their emancipation from parental control is a fait accompli! Such permissiveness, particularly during preadolescence and adolescence, could be detrimental to their future. In spite of all the fictitious, pseudo life-style projected in films and television serials and glossy magazines, female sex in our country, by the large, choose to remain conventional rather than controversial !

Girls realise the sacrifice made by their parents toward their education. They do not while away their time in cafeteria or corridors. They use the library much more than boys. They literally breakdown whenever they receive low grades in class tests. The discomfiture before their classmates would wound their self-esteem. They leave no stones unturned to make up for their loss and toil night and day to improve their performance.

On the contrary, boys, by and large, tend to be lackadaisical, procrastinative and relatively less sensitive to their grades. Most of the boys take pride in declaring they are not book-worms. A good many choose alternate avenues like sports, games and co-curricular activities by devoting disproportionate time and energy. They exude overconfidence and invariably spend midnight oil during examination-time.

Above all, girls are pretty determined to break the myth that they belong to the weaker sex. They are hell-bent on dismantling the male chauvinism and asserting their feminism!

Index

❑❑❑